Readers Praise

GW00729031

"The meditations shoul[...] are going through personal [...] someone close to them, div[...] [...] reassess and reorient their whole lives."

—Margarete Meador, M.D., Psychiatrist

"I believe [*Crisis to Wellness*] could be useful for people who are hurting—people in a situation of change, when their feet seem to be knocked out from under them. Or you can read the meditations as a psychological 'book of common sense' on how to live life. I especially like the section on 'Encounters,' but I think everybody is going to have a favorite set of meditations."

—Stephanie Brown, M.A., Clinical Psychologist

"My work load is cyclical and when it peaks, the pressure to find solutions under fierce deadlines can be overwhelming. It is easy for me to become irritable, agitated, and demanding, making it even more difficult to succeed. Reading [*Crisis to Wellness*] has an immediate calming effect. Petulla's words diffuse my feelings of dire urgency and impending crisis. I am able to relax and work with patient concentration. I can laugh with colleagues, so problems can get solved, and the work becomes fun again."

—Nancy Howe, Computer Professional

"It puts spirituality back into the human person, not outside your ordinary life…but integrated and offering completeness and wholeness, that is, wellness."

—Rev. Stephen Smith, Priest and Counselor

"The book has helped me identify and focus on things that have been troublesome in my life. You don't often find topics like "money" or "projects" in spiritual reading."

—Barbara St. Michaels, M.A.
School District Counselor

"All around me I see people who are searching for a source of inner strength and peace. Our culture suggests they turn to religion, but frequently Sunday sermons offer little consolation or relief. *Crisis to Wellness* illustrates a path by which anyone can begin to live his or her ordinary life in a way that is religious, infused with spirituality and meaning."

—Antonia Girard, Writer

"Unlike much self-help literature, Petulla is not 'pushing' remedies but calling us to reflect on the balance in our lives between actively striving to reach our goals and quietly embracing the unexpected gifts and limits of everyday reality. The aphoristic and anecdotal style opens up 'space' for the reader to meditate in resonance with the author."

—Professor Norman Gottwald, Ph.D.
N.Y. Theological Seminary, Author, *The Tribes of Yahweh*

"Crisis to Wellness provides meditations for people who live active lives but who also want to touch the depths of their being in a new way. It is a wonderful instrument for increasing the quality of one's life through self acceptance."

—James L. Empereur, S.J., Ph.D.
Institute of Spirituality and Liturgy, Jesuit School of Theology

"In our work we have found that a person's attitudes and emotional state play an important role in recovery from many kinds of disease. *Crisis to Wellness* creates a clarity and a sense of optimism. I liked the unusual themes of the book and the discussions of spirituality that are open to many religions."

—Irene Harrison, M.A., Medical Social Worker
Kaiser Permanente Hospitals

"I read *Crisis to Wellness* in the midst of a personal crisis; it helped and comforted me immensely. In reading it I rediscovered certain universal truths illuminating my own path...and providing me with tools to work with my particular situation."

—Lise Teilmann, Office Manager

Crisis
TO
Wellness

MEDITATIONS FOR A PHILOSOPHY OF LIVING

Crisis
TO
Wellness

MEDITATIONS FOR A PHILOSOPHY OF LIVING

JOSEPH PETULLA

COMMUNITY RESOURCE INSTITUTE PRESS
BERKELEY, CALIFORNIA

Community Resource Institute Press
1442-A Walnut Street, #51
Berkeley, California 94709
(510) 525-9663

Published in the United States of America.

First printing: January 1993

ISBN: 0-9628464-2-2

Library of Congress Catalog Card No. 92-74018

Closing the circle: A portion of the proceeds from this book will be used to support reforestry efforts.

Publisher's Cataloging in Publication

Petulla, Joseph M. 1932-
  Crisis to wellness : meditations for a philosophy of living / Joseph Petulla.
    p. cm.
  Includes bibliographical references.
  ISBN 0-9628464-2-2

  1. Self-realization--Religious aspects. 2. Mind-body. 3. Life change events. 4. Spiritual exercises. I. Title.

BF637.S4P48 1993   158.12
                                    QBI92-1760

---

*This book is dedicated
to the memory of my parents,
Louis and Jennie Petulla,
whose gifts of love, generosity,
trust, and example
I cherish with the
fullest measure of gratitude.*

Acknowledgments

I would like to thank Nancy Howe for her friendship and for encouraging me to have these meditations published. Her many, many insightful comments through the stages of preparation have greatly enriched the text.

Many thanks to Bart Brodsky of Community Resource Institute Press for his interest in the book, for suggesting a coherent focus for the manuscript, and for sharpening it in many ways. Bart has amazed me with his understanding of all aspects of the publishing enterprise and has been a joy to work with. Would that all authors could be so lucky! And thanks to Janet Geis for a keen eye on the text and all-round boost in CRIP's production and marketing department.

I would like to thank Harlan Stelmach and Nancee Sobanya of the Vesper Society for their generous and insightful comments in the Foreword. Thanks also for help and comments from Stephanie Guynn, Barbara St. Michaels, and Irene Harrison. And especially to Maggie for the constant love that energizes the wellness of my life.

Contents

Illustration Credits

Foreword

The Chinese symbol for crisis wisely unites two ideas—danger and opportunity. Webster says crisis is "the decisive moment; a turning point; that change is a disease which indicates whether the result is recovery or death." Danger, a turning point, an opportunity—that's what a crisis is.

Crisis to wellness is always a turning point, a signal, an opportunity to pay attention, to watch what is happening to yourself. This experience is what *Crisis to Wellness* describes. The crisis can be an illness, stress, depression, pain, fatigue, anxiety, a feeling of meaningless.

Unfortunately, most of us think we should be well all the time. We think that ill health and the bad side of life should never interfere with our wellness.

Even worse, as Guggenbuhl-Craig writes, "according to the contemporary fantasy of health, we must become whole where wholeness is understood in the sense of perfection.... The slightest defect, the least malfunction must be cured, removed, eradicated." Every day television ads proclaim the same ideal: unless we are perfectly well, something is wrong with us. Actually these images are a barrier to true well being.

Wellness demands the acceptance of all experience—illness, weakness, deficiencies, anger, ecstasy, compassion, love, death, helplessness, distress, pain, strength, joy, absolutely everything.

Wellness calls us to be present to ourselves, to be completely open to our reality as it presents itself, all the good and bad of life. Wellness asks us to allow and accept the truth of who we are. Wellness calls us to hold the totality of our being in compassionate awareness.

Joseph Petulla has given time to attend to the truth of his experience and has hearkened to the call of crisis to wellness. Out of his personal experience of crisis and illness he has explored the meaning of wellness in his own life. He says it simply and personally, sharing who he is, his values, his learnings, his philosophy of living every day as it comes. Confiding his thoughts to us, he speaks to many peoples, touching not only those in crisis, but to all of us who aspire to well being. In a world of such ills as global warming, social/political turmoil, rapid lifestyles, and a universal malaise, Petulla offers a much needed message, encouraging us to meditate on what wellness means personally and in the world.

The intimacy of his meditations on reality, feelings, virtue, fun, and other powerful domains of our lives, directs us to contemplate and embellish his wisdom with our own, and from the very intimacies of our own lives. The openness of his meditations allows us to compose our own *Crisis to Wellness* as we read. His Afterward on religious meditation provides a guide for us to continue on the path of wellness after the book is closed.

Joseph Petulla has offered us a gift. It is a gift to be shared. Read it aloud to a friend. Share it with your children and your elders.

NANCEE SOBONYA, M.A.
Bereavement Coordinator
Vesper Hospice of the East Bay

HARLAN STELMACH, Ph.D.
President and CEO, Vesper Society
Health and Social Services

San Leandro, California

Introduction

In the fall of 1988 I experienced a confusing, un-nerving situation that I had never known before. After dozens of years living a full, energetic life, I was struck down with serious heart disease, and much later I discovered I was also suffering from chronic fatigue syndrome. I had heart surgery, but my condition did not improve despite a faithful adherence to an exercise and diet routine. In fact, after exercising I found I could hardly function at all. Every morning represented a new challenge to muster up the energy to get through the day. Finally, I realized something was radically wrong with my assumptions about my health—and my life.

When I found out I had symptoms of chronic fatigue immune dysfunction syndrome (CFIDS), I learned that exercise aggravates the symptoms. Although I knew my own health problems were not nearly so severe as many people with similar diagnoses, it became apparent to me that no dramatic recovery was in sight. As the months and years dragged on, I became increasingly pessimistic about ever regaining the good health I had once enjoyed. I responded to the problem by trying dozens of highly touted remedies—Eastern and Western—and also examining everything from my diet to the psychological and religious foundations of my life. I spent more and more time reading the classics of literature and religion and reflecting on their themes. I kept a notebook of my thoughts, sometimes based on one of the readings, or more often based on a personal challenge stemming from my health problems. Later I organized the meditations according to the subjects covered in this book.

Illness or any kind of distress may prompt some of us to look inward for causes of our problems, to find what went wrong in the way we were living. Further, we are used to expecting simple, causal relationships in our lives. When we get a headache, we take an aspirin to get rid of it. The more I probed inwardly, the more I uncovered the many factors that influenced the way I felt. I needed to recover the deep psychological and spiritual roots of the way I approached my work and everything else in the world. This book is based on the assumption that there is an intimate, complex connection between our physical, psycho-physical, psychological and spiritual expressions of our lives. I do not assume, however, that tuning up the psychological or spiritual sides will automatically fix a physical problem.

Writing down these thoughts has brought me to one firm conclusion. That focusing on many levels of my life has enabled me to cope with difficulty more easily and disposed me to better physical health. Although I am not yet able to perform many of the physical activities I engaged in before my illness, my life has been greatly enriched because of these meditations.

Furthermore, *Crisis to Wellness* means more than searching for a way out of a serious health problem. Some of us are thrown into small crises every day that loom like giants at the time they occur. Soon we find ourselves in a continual jumpy, irritable frame of mind. These incidents may be symptomatic of a deeper problem. They gnaw away at our core and the simple joys of life we once enjoyed to the point of palpable unwellness, whether or not we develop serious illness. Those closest to us are aware of the problem long before we feel it physically.

The title *Crisis to Wellness* implies that everyone is occasionally unwell in the sense that the balance between our inner and outer lives usually is a little out of phase. In this sense we all need to work continually for deeper integrity of spirit and action. We open ourselves to wellness by developing healthy attitudes of living, working, and playing, as well as cultivating deeper meanings of life and religion.

These meditations are designed for those who feel the need to take a fresh look at the way they are living their lives. Perhaps there is distress from little irritations or a big event that has overwhelmed their sense of well-being. This could be the death of a loved one, a divorce, serious or chronic illness, or loss of a job. Or it could be because one has reached a plateau where something seems wrong or missing in life. It is not unusual to look for relief from the mundane and search for deeper meaning.

A personal philosophy offers intellectual and moral directions toward a better life, in this case toward living well in a holistic sense. "Meditations for a philosophy of living," suggests that we need to reflect on the direction of our lives, so these reflections weave patterns in and out of nine themes of our daily lives: reality, feelings, fun, projects, money, encounters, virtue, hope, religion. The meditations are intended to lead us to explore our personal lives, the internal as well as the external dimensions. They encompass how we relate to and work with everything and everybody around us, and, more important, the forces within us: conflicts, hostility, anger, fear, anxiety, disappointments, failures, aspirations, dreams, love, compassion. It is all too clear to us that the healthy and fulfilling sides of our lives coexist with the painful and destructive themes. We need to embrace both sides of the drama of our everyday lives.

As we begin to think about how we should live our lives we quickly become aware of the difference between traditional Eastern and Western cultures. Eastern cultures are present-oriented and sometimes characterized by passivity, whereas Western societies tend to be future-oriented in their aggressive, purposive economic structures. Eastern religions emphasize the need to empty oneself of all desire in order to live in accordance with the source of all life. Many Western philosophies are goal-driven, fueled by the practice of willed virtue, and perhaps even by anxiety, aggression or fear of failure. But although we make willful decisions every day, can we really control events in our lives? We tend to drive ourselves toward all our goals until we run into the reality wall, experience a personal tragedy, lose a job or have a gut-wrenching experience. We often conclude—sometimes without the tragedy—that life, politics, the world, the "system," are too fixed, too complicated, too exhausting to deal with. So we end up not trying to decide anything, except perhaps which TV programs to watch.

Although it is worth exploring many aspects of Eastern and Western philosophy and religion, working out the details is a never-ending struggle. Since we are human, we have to learn how to choose properly when to attack and when to back off. In short, we must learn how to choose to explore, relate to, work with, and reflect on all aspects of our inner and our external lives.

Yet it is not enough to understand that sometimes we have to set goals, and sometimes we have to smell the roses. In most of our activities we have to learn to be <u>goal-oriented and present-oriented</u> at the same time in the same instance. We must be both content and discontent, to accept our lot in life and at the same time to try to change it, to accept the unchangeable and change those things that can be changed. We must learn how to live with tension and relax at the same time, to learn to be loose while we run to complete one task after another. That's the paradox of living, which I think of as having one foot in Western and one foot in Eastern culture at the same time.

Any movement from crisis to wellness requires courage and optimism, even in the blackness of depression. Henry David Thoreau, the great nineteenth century essayist and nature writer, wrote, "Once in the spring over a hundred acres nearby was burned till the earth was sere and black, but by midsummer this space was clad in a fresher and more luxuriant green than everything around it. Shall we then ever despair? Are we not a sproutland too, after ever so many searings and witherings?" We eventually will recover our integrity, one way or another, as Thoreau's meadow did after the fire, as long as we relax and live with a measure of confidence and courage.

Because my background is steeped in Western culture and thought, these guided meditations probe into the directions and meanings of our lives. They only dip in and out of the mystery of mystic union, into which Eastern religions tend to jump directly without discursive reasoning.

This mystery deep within ourselves reaching as far as the universe stretches, according to wise, holy people, is the point at which all contradictions are resolved. It is fitting, therefore, that an "Afterward" be included which briefly explains the major kinds of religious meditation from Eastern as well as Western traditions. A short bibliography on meditation is appended for those who would like to read more on the subject.

You need not start at the beginning of this book. The themes keep reappearing no matter where you are reading. My hope is that at least a few of these thoughts will touch your life in a way that brings you a fuller measure of wellness.

The most terrifying reality—and the suffering that goes with it—brings a joy of great discovery because it clarifies what we had long suspected but never completely understood.

MARCEL PROUST
Remembrance of Things Past
Cities of the Plain

ONE

Reality

Writer and lecturer Agar N. Jackson once suffered a stroke that left him partially paralyzed and unable to speak. Through a demanding program of physical and speech therapy he eventually was able to live a normal life. One of his favorite stories to illustrate his life came from the history of the sugar maples on his Vermont farm. Over a half-century ago the owner of the property planted the maples because he wanted to use them as posts for barbed wire he strung around his pasture. What was interesting to Mr. Jackson was that some trees accepted the wire into their new growth, while others seemed to fight it. The trees that took in the wire grew straight and tall; the latter became gnarled, disfigured, forever scarred.

Jackson's story of the maples is reminiscent of Eastern philosophy and religion since it suggests a way of moving from crisis to wellness. A wise person in Eastern culture doesn't fight adversity or difficulty head-on, rather accepts as it is, or yields to its power, then works with it toward wellness. We Westerners are more used to fighting evil, or what we think is evil, rooting it out at utmost cost. Complete and utter utopia has never been possible either for individuals or society at large. When we accept the underside of our own personal reality, with courage we can grow straight and tall.

When we are confronted with things we don't like in the world, we sometimes try to fight them with sheer will power alone. We try to take reality by the throat and shake what we want out of it. Often we are successful. When we are not—usually for reasons beyond our control—we turn up the heat and fight harder. At some point we come face-to-face with the massive stone wall of reality. Either we stop and assess the situation and change our goals, or we bash our head against the wall. It's better to accept and work with an immovable object we don't like than to deny its existence, curse it or continue a bloody battle. The will has power but is not omnipotent.

Reality means living everyday life. It is the way we work, play, relate to people, the bottom-line stuff of who we are and what we do. Not what might be, or what we hope it will be, or who we might become someday—richer, more successful, someone with a perfect partner, more obedient children, better working conditions. Our happiness, our future, our maturity depends on how we accept and work with conditions in our everyday lives, the ups and the downs, happiness and sadness, together. The present moment is our reality—conversations with friends and clients, a daily walk, what we see and hear and taste and feel. If we appreciate the present moment, we hardly need more. Such appreciation relaxes our stern view of things, slows us down, brings with it simplicity, contentment and health of mind. Restlessness and impatience signal our need to stop and appreciate what is happening right now.

The foremost fact of reality is that good and bad are tightly interwoven. Living encompasses pleasure and pain, good health and illness, life and death, happiness and sadness, friends and enemies, easy and hard, what might be and what is. Such is the fabric of our lives. To accept and make the best of both sides is the challenge of living. Here's the rub: living life sets up a tension between what is happy, easy, comfortable and what is sad, difficult and uncomfortable. We cannot resolve the tension by running from the unsavory part of life. We should never be surprised by the appearance of difficulty and trouble in our lives. We can relax and enjoy life only by accepting the barbs of reality into our everyday pleasures, as Jackson's maples did.

We expect to be happy most of the time and consider disappointment and pain to be only momentary setbacks. We expect not only to "pursue happiness" as a constitutional right but also to achieve and enjoy its full measure. We tend to block pain and the idea of pain out of our lives, and when difficulty comes, we try to dodge it. We even try to avoid the possibility of pain and unhappiness, running to doctors for sedatives or avoiding the risk of unhappy encounters. We can't seem to learn that we have to grapple with the "downside" of life if we want to enjoy the upside. We have to admit difficulty, live with it, work it out, and prepare for a lifetime of struggle, major and minor. Looking reality in the eye means accepting these tensions and stresses. We never have the "whole ball of wax." We have to adjust to obtaining a few of our many goals, accepting partial solutions to problems along the way.

Henry David Thoreau wrote that "disease is not the accident of the individual, nor even of the generation, but of life itself. In some form, and to some degree or other, it is one of the permanent conditions of life. There is not a lily pad but has been riddled by insects. Almost every shrub and tree has its gall, oftentimes esteemed as its chief ornament and hardly to be distinguished from its fruit. If misery loves company, misery has company enough."

So many wonderful things are woven into our lives—gestures of love, material comforts, work accomplishments, children—we fall into a pattern of expecting everything that happens will be smooth and gentle. Worse, we take the joys for granted. Reality is gratifying and stimulating when we measure the hundreds of moments of happiness we are given compared to the sprinkling of difficulties and pains of life. Reality is joyful when we recognize how much joy and love we have built into our lives.

Sports—especially baseball because there are so many games every year—gives us an accurate prototype of life. It's great when you win, but you can't win them all. You often win on flukes, often lose on flukes, but there's a new game tomorrow. The game is unpredictable, but you can deal with the problems. You can't control everything in the game. You can do a lot to protect your position, bank on good prospects, but you can't control everything. That's the way life is. Nobody can control everything. The rich and powerful fail; the poor and powerless triumph; the healthy get sick. Can you imagine how hard life would be for a baseball player (or a fan for that matter) who has to experience thousands of games and could not accept losing? A good player relishes the wins and knows how to accept losses because there's another game tomorrow.

Today is a new day. At some point we must forget about yesterday. It had its sorrows and joys, bad feelings and good feelings, blunders and good work, embarrassments and high points, insensitive and compassionate moments. Today should be enjoyed with the joy of anticipation, not burdened with ghosts of yesterday's perceived failures. Reality is now and should not be burdened down with yesterday's nonsense. Once we have learned a lesson it is time to move on.

The most insidious words of any language are "if only…." If only this had happened or that hadn't happened. Or "what if this had happened." "If I had gotten that job, or not gotten sick." "If only this or that would happen, I know I'd be happy." These possibilities are mere figments of the imagination even if they are common expectations. The horrible, seemingly unlikely tragedies—random shootings or quirky accidents that cause so much suffering—happen just as surely as coming home to dinner. And gifts of life come out of the blue, maybe after someone works for a lifetime on a goal but never really expects it. Reality is what happens to people and what people make happen. The only true certainty is that life is unpredictable, filled with big and little crises. Still, crises can be diffused into balance and wellness.

The Irish poet Seamus Heaney has written, "The best music is the music that is playing." That is, not music (or reality) that is still imagined, or music we hope will play, or music we want to be played, or any other kind of music. We can best enjoy the music that is being played, and if we want some other music to play, we can do whatever is possible to bring it out of our imagination. Then it will become the best music because it is playing, and if it is _not_ playing we can enjoy the best music that _is_ playing.

It is always uncertain what we can change in ourselves or in society. In western society we have the strong notion that we can do anything, always keep good health, eliminate poverty, change people's attitudes, become rich and famous, if only we work hard enough. The reality we experience is not always ready to be changed. We have to work with what we have, with the limitations of other people and social conditions. Of course, we can't give up because we don't know our limits. We just have to do our best and not build excessive expectations.

It doesn't work just to go with the flow, to stay laid back and enjoy life, ignoring its underside. We could never find our niche or level of development if we didn't push against our limits, do our level best in work and play. On the other hand, we can't manipulate reality as though we could mold it at will. We have to work with what's there, look for the right time to act, test the waters, but never be so sure we can control events. Since we can't dictate everything that happens to us, we might as well try to relax while we work for our better tomorrow.

If we want comfortable lives, we get in the habit of running from difficulty, from people who challenge us, from projects that might fail, or any other kind of risk of life. Yet we have to keep reminding ourselves that the road to fulfillment is not a gradual slope with no potholes, but one with sudden turns and unexpected bumps.

Acceptance of reality is critical in both psychology and religion. This includes accepting all of our own deepest feelings as well as those of others. We assume that we should be perfect, and that being perfect means we are always sweetness and light. We even assume people may hate us, or lose respect for us, if we show an "unfriendly" emotion. Perfectionism is the enemy of accepting ourselves as we are. Perfectionism won't allow us to assume we may be average, fitting into the commonplace scheme of things, or even appearing a little unsavory.

Acceptance of our total selves as we are, with all our eccentricities in the world we live, is the foundation of inner peace. We should learn to enjoy our own little quirks, laugh at ourselves. This helps diffuse the daily tensions of living. Then we are able to live life with minimal fear and see the loveliness of the world around us.

Much of what we are is determined by our genetic code, but we don't know the limits of that code.

We may be chastened by disability but could govern the country in difficult times as Franklin Roosevelt has done. We may overcome seemingly insuperable health problems to astound the world of physics, as Stephen Hawking has done. Our genes may or may not dispose us to cancer or alcoholism, but we don't have to smoke or drink to compound the difficulty. We might have a history of bad hearts in our families, but we don't have to eat fat or sugar, and we can exercise. We don't have to live perfect lives. Ordinary lives can be finessed into something pretty good. We shouldn't be deluded by the ad people into becoming someone other than who we are.

We rarely know what the truly significant events are in our lives: the person who will change our lives; the book that will provide a stunning insight; the study that leads us to a new career. Or the tragedy that turns our lives into something meaningful. We only can cultivate the habit of being open to all the events of our lives and be ready to act on their message.

To develop the habit of acceptance of reality means we accept our lives: who we are and what happens to us along the way. This does not mean we should be smug about ourselves or do not need to change what we can change. We do not know what we can change in our lives and should not expect ourselves to change everything. We only can set a few goals, do our best according to our own best judgment and not expect things to become perfect for ourselves or our situations. Perfectionism undermines all our efforts for healthy, realistic changes in ourselves and our lives. We hold onto unlikely notions that we should accomplish every goal, finish every humanitarian project. We don't want to be quitters, but sometimes we should back off.

The culture has imprinted its definition of a "loser" on everybody's consciousness: failure, stigma, someone with no value. Only the "successful" need apply—for jobs, for praise, for a claim to self-worth. So when we don't publicly succeed, when others don't recognize our efforts, when we don't achieve our goals, however unrealistic, we rationalize, become defensive, try to hide the loss. We feel it to the quick, often fall into a crisis.

Losing packs a punch. It doesn't matter whether we lose something—money, a game—personally or because we identify with the loser like the hometown team. The feeling of loss sticks like glue until we somehow shake it. "Those bums should'a never lost," we pout, hoping to talk ourselves out of a funk. Why do we persist in thinking we, or our allies, should never lose? Personal immaturity? An immature culture that cannot admit the thought of losing?

Some people seem to lose far more than they win and know very well that losing—the barbed wire in the maples—is a great part of their lives. What they need—what we all need in a losing streak—is to muster courage, put bitterness aside, and refrain from blaming fate or others for our problems. Then we can move on with dignity, standing tall.

Loss is built into everything we are and do—our health, our control over our destinies, what we want versus what we can do. We have some control over our health if we eat and live right, but some people are genetically disposed to specific diseases. Viruses attack even the healthy. Do we expect to be healthy all our lives, to put off death forever? Loss is built into life. The consoling fact is that winning is also built into life if our idea of winning is beyond what the culture pounds into us, i.e., merely fame and fortune.

Reality is partly controlled by what we believe, what we think is worth-while, how we choose to live with what we have. Reality is also what we make of things, and especially how we develop ourselves in our hearts and minds. It depends on what we choose to read, how we look at the world and the people around us, what thoughts we choose to think. Our genetic backgrounds, home and cultural environments modify a great deal, but at bottom we are choosing our own lives.

First we need to accept who we are and what we have so we can enjoy our daily lives. Then we need to set realistic goals of education, career and surroundings, so we can make our lives and the lives of those around us even happier. Most of all we have to listen to our feelings and be honest about them. What do we want for ourselves? What can we realistically do? What do we really need? Are we on a course which will fulfill these needs?

Reality is now. We can plan for the future but should not live in it. An old definition of contentment is drinking the *contents* of a cup. We should not avoid drinking the contents because we only have half a cup at the moment, or because taste isn't absolutely perfect, or because we don't like the looks of the cup. If we did, we would be cheating ourselves out of the enjoyment of what we have, which is quite a bit, and end up being *discontented*.

All religions portray the deepest level of human existence in divine terms: for Buddhism, we uncover Buddha or God-life; for Taoism, the Tao or the divine Way; Hinduism, Brahman or God; for Christianity, the soul, the seat of grace or divine life. Religious myths narrate the myriad ways, evils, obstacles, barriers to be overcome before we reach the divine treasure. Jesus says we must lose our life to find it. In religion we find stories of people who have preceded us in this ultimate reality of life.

When we accept the total reality of life, the reality within us and without, we enter a world of thousands of further decisions, mostly unclear ones, problematic, sometimes right, sometimes wrong. In religious terms, accepting the total reality of life leads us to choosing the "Way" or Tao, or in Christian terms, the Logos that gives us Life.

Thoreau saw divine joy woven into every living being. He said, "Think of the young fish leaping in ponds, the incessant song of the tree toad with which the woods ring in the spring, the nonchalance of the butterfly carrying accident and change painted in a thousand hues upon its wings, or the brook minnow stoutly stemming the current, the luster of whose scales worn bright is reflected on the bank. Open all your pores and bathe in all the tides of nature, in all her streams and oceans, at all seasons." If all nature contains defects and disease within itself, it also constantly flashes bright and jumps for joy. Living, the saying goes, is like licking honey off a thorn.

Feeling a tremendous rakehell, and not liking myself much for it, and feeling rather a good chap for not liking myself much for it, and not liking myself at all for feeling rather a good chap.

KINGSLEY AMIS
That Uncertain Feeling

TWO

Feelings

*N*ancy Mairs *is a writer, wife, mother and has had multiple sclerosis for almost 20 years. She needs help walking, tying her shoes, caring for bodily needs and for hundreds of other things most of us never think about. She wrote a book entitled* Carnal Acts *which illustrates how her feelings, even her self-identity, is fixed into her body. She writes, "I call myself a cripple...because the word is the most accurate and precise I've found...."*

At the end of the book she describes a trip to visit her daughter, a Peace Corps volunteer in Africa, despite self-doubts and a Luftansa agent reluctant to sell her a ticket. She struggled getting around, walking a little, using her wheelchair, and being carried by Zairians. But get around she did, to out-of-the-way outhouses, markets, and even to a harvest of locally grown fish. At the end of her essay, she tells of the bittersweet moment of exultation when, leaving the airport, she realized that would be her "last glimpse of Africa: the dilapidated airport..., sunlight glancing from the fronds of feather palms, in the distance Kinshasa's few tall buildings against an opalescent sky, the whole view blurred by tears...."

'What if I'd never come? I ask myself. How could I bear never to have seen this?' "

Happiness starts with how we look at ourselves. Feelings are our happiness gauge, how we handle insecure feelings, fear, anxiety, feelings of hurt, as well as good feelings of pleasure or satisfaction. These emotions most of all depend on how we accept and appreciate ourselves and our "body-feelings." Self-rejection of any feeling is often the source of a deep personal crisis. It can lead to psychological insecurity and a hostility that often is projected onto others. Or it can cause a person to create a false personality in order to deal with people in everyday life.

It is not easy for us to look deeply into ourselves, to try to understand why we react the way we do. We're so used to protecting ourselves by defensive actions and remarks, or projecting feelings we deny onto other people, that we sincerely see no need to examine ourselves. Sometimes it takes a great personal shock—a heart attack, cancer, a loss, an accident—to push us into examining our deeper feelings. If it takes a catastrophe to force us to look into ourselves, then that crisis is in part a lucky event.

Jesus said that the kingdom of God is within ourselves. That is, God resides in every corner of our emotions, mind, and spirit. Human nature might not always show itself as good—it is aggressive, defensive, malicious, and sometimes violent. Good and evil feelings within ourselves cause a tension that strives to be resolved. With calm acceptance of the stress, we have discovered the first clue we need to resolve the crises, i.e., looking within ourselves, without fear.

Jesus and many others have emphasized we have to love others as we love ourselves. We cannot love others unless we love ourselves first. We have to look into our own needs and satisfy them, not try to live a life of utter sacrifice as though we don't matter personally. Sometimes playing the role of a saint can cover up an insecure person who feels worthless and actually is self-centered and selfish. That is, we work for others more to solicit favorable comment rather than because we are challenged by a higher calling. Whatever we do should begin with a healthy sense of our own worth, interests, and good or bad points.

What should we do with unfriendly feelings— fear or fear of failure, anxiety, discouragement, depression, mood swings, feelings of hurt from insults, betrayal, anger? What <u>can</u> we do with them? Play them out? Go on an emotional binge? Root them out? Deny them? They hang on, despite our best efforts. However difficult, we have to experience them and <u>let them pass</u>—they always do—and not try to beat them down by act of the will. All feelings are the most explicit proof of our humanity, our physical and emotional conflicts, our limitations as well as our strengths and enjoyment. Most of us never adjust to the idea that bad feelings are a true part of our personalities and need to be accepted as such.

In the face of unfriendly feelings we need to conjure up some friendly feelings. This could be a positive thought about someone, cuddling a loved one, thinking of a happy moment, or remembering a religious feeling. Unfriendly feelings are not big events in the scheme of things. They might want to do a little damage, wake us up to something, and then flit away. Thus we need not be upset by them. A little love or friendship is just as much a part of us as sadness or anger, so we might be able to turn a bad feeling into a good one. One thing we know for sure is that feelings come and go, bad and good, even when in conflict with each other. We have to <u>acknowledge their presence</u>, but we don't have to be dragged into their emotional maelstrom.

Depressive feelings are like unstable molecules. They want to combine with something: an outburst, a recognition of their being, an action, or even be converted to a friendly feeling. It is sometimes possible to transfer a feeling of disappointment to a desire to do something positive. A feeling of stress can become a feeling of peace or tranquillity. Anger can be dissipated and transformed by strenuous physical activity like running, cycling, or weightlifting. Most of all we should not blame ourselves for having "bad" feelings. We know the opposite happens—friendly feelings turning to unfriendly ones—so we might want to observe in ourselves how unfriendly can flip over into friendly feelings.

Thoreau noted mood swings in himself when he said, "No wonder that so many commit suicide, life is so barren and worthless; we only live on by an effort of the will. But our condition suddenly changes in a flash, and even the barking of a dog is a pleasure to us. So closely is our happiness bound up with our physical condition, one reacts on the other."

When we experience the death of a loved one or an unhappy incident that arouses tension or stress, we have to learn to accept the feelings as real. Then we can let go. We need to step away from the situation, not force the issue, and say to ourselves, "It's OK; I'm alright; no damage; we'll move on." Hopefully, our feelings will follow our thoughts. Happy or positive thoughts without inner feelings won't turn the tide, but it is our responsibility to try at least to conjure up the friendly thought. That is, we can act: call a friend, talk through the feelings, go for walks or a run, get a project we can throw ourselves into. Positive thinking in itself cannot change an uncomfortable situation but it is a good start.

The practitioners of Eastern meditation say, "A silent mind is all you need." The mind quiets itself, letting all feelings come and go, and just watches what happens. The peaceful mind doesn't interpret what's going on, doesn't make harsh or friendly judgments about one's anger or greed or envy or love or compassion. It becomes only a silent witness of the life of the feelings and lets them come and go. In silent meditation we can simply observe and release feelings of tension in the body. By practicing this kind of meditation some people are freed of fear of their emotions, their conflicts, sometimes of bad health itself.

If we experience unfriendly feelings regularly, we may begin to fear them. Or worse, we develop a pattern of reacting, then hating ourselves for giving in to a "bad" habit. The habit, fed by fear, becomes more ingrained. The cycle continues to make matters worse. Aren't depressive feelings part of our nature? Even more, aren't they completely within our character? We Westerners deny this reality and assume we can live without sad or hurtful feelings. Nobody exists with only "heavenly" desires and emotions.

The challenges of personal growth bring on their own fears and anxiety. These include a new step in life, a new job, confronting demons in ourselves, like drinking or drugs. We are anxious and depressed because we lack the courage to make the step forward. If we do not, we fix ourselves in an immature state of growth. We need to face the causes of our fear in order to pass through the crisis.

Sometimes a public (or even private) outburst leads to feelings of sadness when we realize that we can't control our antisocial (impolite) feelings. We think we should be beyond this kind of behavior. Both sides of the syndrome are difficult. We can't seem to control our wayward impulses, which seem to be completely uncalled for. Neither can we pull out of the guilt feelings of sadness afterward, which sap all the joy out of living. It helps to accept ourselves and other people. Since we know we act this way with no bad will (unless we indulge in justifying our outbursts), we can understand many other people who have the same problem. The more we accept the rocky part of our human nature, the less perfectionist we become, and the less we expect ourselves and others to be perfect in every way.

Many studies show that daily irritations are partial causes of heart and other problems. Hassles at work, fretting over injustices both real and imagined, conflicts at home and on the job, and other worries such as a loved one's death, are predictors of illness. We have to know there is a way out of minor and major irritations, that we can understand our own reactions and help ourselves out of them.

When we are in the middle of a funk, we tend to focus on troubles, problems, abilities we lack. We all possess many more abilities and gifts of life we never think about. Why is it so hard to remember how fortunate we really are? It's a good practice to try to figure out which of our abilities, friends, and possessions are the best, then realize how much we would be deprived without these gifts of life. More than anything we have to remind ourselves to appreciate how much we have going for us. Physical and psychological wellness fills as much of our life as crisis does.

It's possible that we will begin to feel the way we are acting. So if we feel sad or irritable, we can play the role of a comic. We can try to smile, i.e., smile at our own poor jokes, silliness, at the faces and frolicking of children, and tapping into our memories of favorite funny stories. When we are in the middle of a funk, this may be the hardest antidote of all. Feeling good often follows acting good, so our well-being might be restored with a wide, wide smile. The point is we can decide to adopt another posture or feeling. We can interrupt the negative flow of energy within ourselves and begin to replace it with a positive flow.

Some people get the flow going at the start of the day by paying bridge tolls for the cars behind them or buying donuts for co-workers. They look for ways to enhance their own spirit as well as other people's.

Hard (as opposed to soft) feelings are a part of life. We cannot escape them. We cannot insulate ourselves from them. We cannot run from them or close our eyes to them any more than we can escape or run from the difficulties that accompany everything else in life. By facing them calmly and with courage, we nurture confidence and growth. We develop a resilience, both a soft and a hard side, Yin and Yang according to the ancient Eastern thinkers.

Calming down in the middle of an emotional storm can be the most difficult process in life. We need not become upset when we are not successful in a small task. At any time in the cycle of an unfriendly feeling, we simply can choose not to be upset. We are easily caught up in an explosion of feelings that carry us away. Sooner or later, with or without our cooperation, the emotion passes and we can think and act more clearly. It may take a lifetime of practice to achieve a semblance of imperturbability under stress, "to accept with serenity the things that cannot be changed," and to develop "the courage to change the things that can be changed."

Why do we expect to control all difficulties or hard feelings? Whatever gave us the idea that this is possible even part of the time? Maybe it's built into Western culture, or Western religion. Maybe we hold to the Christian idea that the cross (accepting pain or difficulty) is supposed to be over quickly. We think that our true Christian situation should always be with the joyous, triumphant, resurrected Christ. Eastern religions seem to hold a deeper truth: that evil is always with us, just as good is. The question of why God allows evil to afflict good people would never occur to a Buddhist. Taoists affirm we have to learn to balance the good and the evil in life. Maybe we should look for other views of the Christ experience on earth. Or understand that Christianity has been changed from the traditional understanding of the need to accept pain with our joy. The modern view blinks at evil and accepts only a vision of the comfortable life.

Maybe emotional volatility is strictly physical, located at the base of the brain, the R-complex, which evolved hundreds of millions of years ago and which we share with reptiles. Or with the limbic system, the seat of emotions which surrounds the R-complex, which we share with other mammals. When we perceive a threat, we often react as our ancestral reptiles would react: fight or flight without pause. The backwash of the reaction stays with us, and we try to justify what we did, or are ashamed of it. No need to panic. We only need to use the thinking part, the neocortex (which we share with other advanced mammals), to calm ourselves down and try to repair the damage to ourselves or others. Life is sometimes messy, in part at least, because our brain is so complicated.

If we nurture the angry or panicky 'fight or flight' response, it can stay with us in our memory indefinitely and we will continue to suffer its torments. The feeling of anger or hurt then begins to control other sides of our life. It pushes out love, compassion, joy. It's far better to come to terms with our behavior, forgive a slight, and change the emotional pattern into opposite feelings.

The Tao Te Ching speaks about the wise man who knows enough to let himself calm down when he is upset. Stirred-up, muddy waters will eventually settle and clear up after a while. When we are stirred up, maybe perturbed because of the way we are acting or feeling, we should think: calm, calm, calm. Wait for the waters to clear.

"That was hard to digest, hard to swallow." This is how we say our feelings have difficulty adjusting to an everyday hurt, insult, trauma, loss. Many things are hard to swallow but can be taken with a little buffering agent, i.e., a calm reckoning of the situation. Maybe things will change for the better. They usually do, don't they?

ιenever we become upset from any source—
ιy congestion, unfair traffic ticket, insulting
coworker, unaffectionate spouse—it is helpful to
examine the source of the feeling and understand it.
Sometimes we can help ourselves just by deciding to
do or feel something else. Just because freeway
traffic is unpleasant does not mean we have to be
upset every time we go out in it.

The deeper we probe into our consciousness, the
more we will learn about ourselves and why we
react in certain ways. We should not be too proud to
examine our values and beliefs, even our religious
beliefs, as well as defensive reactions to other people.
What do we think is important,? What is our place in
the world? Why do we usually become angry in a
certain situation? Why do feelings of depression
arise in certain situations? We need to get to the
bottom of our feelings, with or without the help of
other people. Moreover, we need to be utterly honest
with ourselves.

The French expression, *le petit bonheur*, "the little
happiness" or "little pleasures," expresses what all
of us experience every day—little feelings of joy
found in commonplace things. We should learn to
recognize them quickly, freeze them, and put them
into our memories, maybe onto our calendars for
future enjoyment. Enjoy every act of generosity or
love: a loved one's expression, an accomplishment,

completing a task, fun at a wedding, a friend's gratitude, savoring a spring day. There are thousands of feelings of pleasure etched in our memories but rarely visited. One does not need to be a king, millionaire, or president to be rich in the small pleasures of life.

We savor the little pleasure after something happens or when we notice something beautiful for the first time. The joy often comes because it is completely unexpected, an act of grace coming out of nowhere: an empty parking place, a pat on the back, a great meal. These moments can more than make up for problems, defeats or setbacks we suffer. We simply need to catch the little piece of joy, in midair, as it were, or even reflect on the moment much later. We have to get in the habit of seeing pleasures and defeats as intertwined with the good of living.

For Nancy Mairs, the extraordinary difficulty of coping with life in Zaire was balanced by the split-second joy of seeing Africa for the last time and feeling the experience of being there. Stress and difficulty became near-ecstasy mixed with a realization that she almost missed a great event in her life.

One of the deepest joys of life is intimacy, the closeness we feel toward a loved one, the feeling of being loved. It brings the mutual trust and personal security that comes from a lifetime of sharing and openness. We need to share and acknowledge the joy of intimacy so we don't take it for granted.

There are so many things we have done in our lives that have brought us pleasure. There are experiences with family and friends, foods we ate as children, ethnic history, music we have played and loved…. We have within ourselves billions of bits of memory that could cheer any day. We need to get out old pictures and look at them from time to time to revive these memories.

Nature is a wonderful source of pleasure when we notice it. How happy our dog is to see us when we come home, yelping, dancing, wagging its tail—or a cat purring on our lap. It is hard not to enjoy these moments of animal encounter. Or simply the majestic sight of a wilderness spread out before us on a drive or a hike; a full moon; a spectacular sunset. We need a moment to let the experience sink in, to concentrate on a wonderful field of pleasure.

As we grow up we find places of relaxation and enjoyment, places we go to avoid the stresses of life. There is that place we once shared with a friend; a place we gained an insight; the place we met our beloved or grew in love together. When we think of or return to these places, the heart stirs in appreciation.

Music is a source of joy to us. When we hear a record of a favorite tune, or a sound that represented an age we relished, we can enjoy the period. When recollections of embarrassment or hurt return to us, we need to return to these happy memories of sound for emotional revival. Ayurvedic medicine teaches that certain kinds of music and smells resonate with patterns within ourselves to enhance well-being. We know that experiencing sound, taste, and touch can cheer us up. We should open ourselves to experiences in the real world which provide the possibility of real joy.

Experiences with old friends and family are a lifeline of support and joy. They are innumerable, a treasure trove of *bonheur*. Death and separation may remove them from us, but their love and the memory of our lives together can remain with us as a source of joy, even with the pain of separation.

We enjoy waiting for a friend, seeing him or her approach. Or as we watch children at play, when they are growing up, responding to our interest and attention. The amazing variety of people, their faces, cultural heritage and expressiveness can draw awe and pleasure from us.

Fun, dancing, subtle jokes, slapstick, games bring pleasure when we are engaged with other people, and smiles when we think or talk about them afterward. It's a good idea to remember happy times, when fun is turned into a moment of pleasure.

Falling in love is a wonderful feeling to remember. With people, cities, children, cats, dogs, cuddly critters, the mountains, redwood trees. It's always a sweet feeling, one of life's most precious. But these feelings come and go. We're sad when they go but they always leave a warm and wonderful memory. We're not just falling in love with love. There is a treasure of memory beneath the emotion, which can stay with us throughout our whole lives.

Teach us delight in simple things,
And mirth that has no bitter springs.
                    RUDYARD KIPLING
                    The Children's Song

THREE

Fun

*E*very year as a counterpoint to the Rose Bowl Parade in Pasadena, an unruly group of citizens march in a mini-extravaganza they call the Doo Dah Parade. Perennial favorites of the occasion are the Marching Precision Brief Case Drill Team (bankers from Pasadena who swing brief cases in unison), the Newport Beach Dull Men's Club (businessmen who march in time to the cacophony of their portable leaf blowers), and housewives pushing outrageous contraptions as though they were shopping carts. There are also hundreds of other wild and crazy individuals and groups dressed in assorted and colorful regalia. It's a loose and cheerful affair, both for participants and viewers, and a good time is had by all.

The Doo Dah Parade began as the Pasadena artist community's reaction to the extreme formality, and occasional pomposity, of the Rose Bowl Parade. The Rose Bowl

Parade is beautiful and sometimes breathtaking but cannot be described as fun. The Doo Dah parade is a lot of fun, a good symbol of the human need to relieve tension and stress, to bring our spirit back into healthy balance. It's a natural phenomenon, maybe like positive and negative electrical charges building up in a cloud that burst forth in lightning and thunder.

If we get too mired in everyday life we fall into a rut. We live out the same role of dominance or submission, of controlling or appearing helpless. Sooner or later this leads us to become burned out or terminally bored. The Doo Dah Parade is a creative reaction to living in a rut. Here one can live out a silly fantasy or make fun of the silliness of being a little too straight-laced the rest of the time.

San Francisco has its own version of the Doo Dah Parade in a benefit race every year, The Bay to Breakers. This is a combination serious and fun run from downtown to the Pacific Ocean. One-hundred-fifty thousand participants join in the event, many of them in hilarious dress, or any dress whatsoever. One team features twenty runners who are attached together and run as a centipede. Hundreds more dress up as famous figures, and every year the run becomes a little more flamboyant. Serious runners have to run first while others are jammed to the point of immobility. The goal is to have fun, finish the race, and get a tee shirt memorializing a great time.

Having fun is sometimes serious business. In the 1970's Norman Cousins often told the story of his collagen illness, a painful and near-fatal disease of the connective tissue, when his joints literally became unstuck. Cousins had read research that indicated adrenal exhaustion could be caused by emotional exhaustion. Since a large part of his medical problem was malfunctioning adrenal glands, Cousins tried to reverse negative feelings in his body. He believed the exhaustion could be causing negative chemical changes leading to his illness, which he wanted to reverse with positive feelings and emotions. Along with large doses of vitamin C, Cousins set up a systematic program to divert himself with laughter. Among other techniques, he watched old Candid Camera and Marx Brothers films, and read joke books. He found that ten minutes of solid belly laughter provided a solid two hours of sleep without pain. When the pain returned, he switched the projector back on. Eventually his disease went into remission, despite a bad prognosis, and Cousins spent the rest of his life explaining the many ways mental attitudes can influence the course of a person's disease. All of us know the therapeutic effects of a hearty laugh. It's amazing we don't try to enjoy life more than we do.

Cousins told stories of how Albert Schweitzer set a tone of joy and companionship with his staff at his hospital in Africa. Music also energized the doctor himself and his community. He also wrote often that the entire history of medicine acknowledged that a merry heart is the best doctor, as theBible says. He quotes Sir Francis Bacon on the need for mirth in one's life. Cousins takes his readers on a trip through history showing every major thinker stressing the importance of humor for good health and a happy life. Cousins himself said that long before he became ill he was convinced that positive emotions could promote good health. Yet, Cousins, as do many of us, needed to be powerfully motivated before acting on this insight.

It seems certain that positive feelings of joy are related to good health. Even a hug or petting a cat or a dog can lower the pulse and boost the immune response. A person with untreatable serious illness can greatly improve his or her quality of life with a positive mental attitude. Cousins speaks of a doctor with terminal cancer who continued to work with his patients because it was something that continued to give him pleasure. He also told of members of a family who took turns researching and telling funny stories to an invalid daughter. The joy of these occasions changed the entire atmosphere and quality of life of the house. We all know disabled people who live with more joy, optimism, and energy than the people who pity them. Despite the pressure of illness or difficulty, it actually is possible to look on the bright side of life, to find occasion to have fun, to laugh. Radio commentator John Hockenberry likes to use his seven-year old niece's definition of his own crippling paralysis: a person who is "not afraid to be stung by bees."

Still, like Norman Cousins, many of us need to be jump-started into learning to "lighten up," with or without serious illness. Maybe we are under the stress of deadlines or a hectic life. Maybe we seem to be tired all the time, possibly suffering from clinical depression and only want to sleep or watch television. Maybe we are so used to working we don't know what to do with free time when it comes along, or maybe we have a hard time sleeping at night. Most of all we might feel as if we're in a rut. These are signs we need to relearn how to have fun, to substitute the pain of stress with joy and relaxation.

If we accept the fact of difficulty and stress in everyday life without getting overly upset, we also need to realize that our lives deserve at least as much fun as stress. We need a Do Dah Parade of our own every once in a while. <u>Having fun is the ability to let go, to be spontaneous, and to let loose of controls.</u> It means to enjoy something so completely that we forget our stresses, what time it is, and lose ourselves in some activity or person. We become kids again. Time stops for us, so we can forget our problems for a while, and when we get back to them they seem less ominous, easier to cope with. Our whole "body-spirit" is relaxed, changed for the better. We are refreshed, rejuvenated.

Many of us relax or have fun only when we can justify the activity, like taking up golf or tennis for recreation to promote good health. We tend to read only articles that help us professionally, or improve our minds—all for pragmatic reasons, not for the sake of pure spontaneous fun. Why do so many of us find it difficult to justify having fun without mixing in some educational or financial goal? Why do we want to spend so much free time moonlighting? Why is it so hard for us to relax when we finally do go on vacation? Or want to spend our vacations on a different kind of work around the house? The answers to these questions are within us and could take months to years to figure out.

Society has given play a bad name, as in "playboy," or "play hooky," both words connoting irresponsibility. The implication is that serious citizens do not 'play around' in life; our culture values work and making money more than anything else, especially having fun. In an era when many of us have to work harder to make ends meet, it is even more important to think about our quality time. We all need to discover the kinds of activities that re-create our spirit.

It could be that we are afraid to let ourselves go, or miss a financial opportunity. We might think having fun is wasting time, or even that we don't want to look like fools. We don't want people to laugh at us and we're afraid to laugh at ourselves. Maybe we should first practice by learning to laugh at our own foibles. Embarrassing mistakes are the first sign of human life. For our own good we should not be afraid to make mistakes, or worry about making fools out of ourselves. We cannot be so controlled or perfect that we are immune from making mistakes. Neither should we spend our time trying to avoid criticism or embarrassment, thereby curbing the ability to lighten our spirit. It is deadening to worry about how we look or might appear to other people. The preoccupation with conforming to a social norm can lead to repressing our more authentic inner self, a process that can make it more and more difficult to relax. Human wellness requires spontaneity, joy, and honest expression of feelings, no matter what other people think.

Having fun means we're comfortable with ourselves, that we accept ourselves, are happy with who we are and satisfied with how we look. We are not perfect and shouldn't want to appear to be. We need to like other people and ourselves. Then we can relax and open our minds and hearts to the present moment, the only one that really counts. We can laugh at our uptight, super-serious side and see what's funny around us. We can let unpleasantness bounce off us. We can enjoy living in the world.

"To have fun" in Italian is *"divertirsi,"* that is

"diverting ourselves," losing ourselves in the moment, delighting in something that's happening. Not the same things are funny or "diverting" for everybody. Games and sports are fun for many people; others don't enjoy them until they are so good they can compete professionally. Then winning becomes so important that the game loses its quality to divert or relax. Professional athletes know the difference. They often say, "It was fun out there today," or "I was completely lost in the game. It didn't even matter whether we won or not!" Play means we become refreshed whether we win or lose.

Many people believe they need to have a few drinks, or take pills or drugs, before they can loosen up. Even if we didn't become addicted or have hangovers, we shouldn't need to take something to assure a good time for ourselves. There are dozens of funny stories every morning in the newspaper, many that are not even intended to be funny. And everywhere we go, people are trying to get us to laugh. They wear weird clothing, make-up, ear or nose rings, color and cut designs in their hair. They tell jokes and put on performances at work and home. Kids are always ready to get a rise out of us. We just have to open our eyes and shouldn't need a half dozen drinks to get a good laugh.

On the other hand, sometimes we might want to tease someone who does not feel like playing. Playful—sometimes crude—remarks can easily be interpreted as insensitivity. They may be a form of sexual harassment, which is one person "making fun" of another rather than "having fun" with him or her. Even these mistakes can help us understand the need to relax. If we apologize for an unintentional insult, we can appreciate the importance of equality and mutuality in fun.

No two people will react to the same situation in the same way. Fun is determined by genes, upbringing, personal values, beliefs and our own unique personalities. Norman Cousins loved the Marx Brothers; we might prefer Woody Allen. (Remember the scene in *Take Money and Run* where Woody is trying to rob a bank? He passes a note to the teller which says "I have a gun" and the teller says, "Let me see, this note says I have a gub." Woody gets into an argument with the teller, pointing to the *n*, saying that couldn't be a *b*. In the meantime a line forms behind him and he gets arrested. Later, when two gangs show up to rob the same bank, the customers are asked to indicate by their applause which gang they would prefer to be robbed by.) We all have different responses to different stimuli, but we need to be disposed to accept the stimuli. Some people crave to jump 200 feet tied to a bungee cord, others love to sit and talk with family and friends in their back yards, or enjoy a long meal with them. But we know that variety is the spice of having fun.

Books or events that guarantee to bring us "fun" rarely work out. It can be artificial to mix fun with cooking, fun at the mall, fun at the theater, fun at the carnival, or fun with philosophy. Purveyors of fun know we are desperate for relaxation and mix it with high-minded activities or pretty girls to make it seem that fun can be dispensed with a spoon. This kind of fun is confused with momentary private pleasure, a form of distraction and escape. It is too superficial to create any lasting enjoyment.

Another quality that goes with fun is that it sneaks up on us, surprises us with delight. The writer or the problem-solver starts out the idea of doing some work and somewhere along the way he or she is giggling at what was created. We start a conversation with some friends and end up laughing our heads off. On the other hand, we can carefully plan a day of fun that ends up a disaster. The unpredictability of fun, like life, is one of its greatest joys. Therefore those who do not have the spirit of adventure miss out because we have to take some risks and be ready for misfortune to gain the fortune of fun. We have to be ready to lose, throw ourselves into the action, and be ready to take delight in anything that comes our way. We cannot force play into a mold. Calculated "play therapy" seems more like "work" therapy than having fun.

In the Myth of Sisyphus, the hero is forced to roll a stone up a hill repeatedly for all eternity. So what if Sisyphus played a game with the stone every time he rolled it up the hill, dancing with it, juggling it, playing soccer with it, and so on? Would his condemnation be so severe?

Mark Twain gives us a classic description of play in his *Adventures of Tom Sawyer*. Tom's Aunt Polly seemingly destroys his day by telling him he has to whitewash their huge fence:

"Tom took up his brush and went tranquilly to work. Ben Rodgers hove in sight presently—the very boy, of all boys, whose ridicule he had been dreading. Ben's gait was the hop-skip-and-jump-proof enough that his heart was light and his anticipations high. He was eating an apple, and giving a long, melodious whoop, at intervals, followed by a deep-toned ding-dong-dong, ding-dong-dong, for he was personating a steamboat. As he drew near, he slackened speed, took the middle of the street, leaned far over to starboard and rounded to ponderously and with laborious pomp and circumstance—for he was personating the *Big Missouri*, and considered himself to be drawing nine feet of water. He was boat and captain and engine-bells combined, so he had to imagine himself standing on his own hurricane-deck giving the orders and executing them: ...Stop the stabboard! Ting-a-ling-ling! Stop the labboard! Come ahead on the stabboard! Stop her! Let your outside turn over slow! ...Come-out with your spring-line—what're you about there! Take a turn round that stump with the bight of it! Stand by that stage, now—let her go! Done with the engines, sir! Ting-a-ling-ling! *Sh't! Sh't!* (trying the gaugecocks)."

"Tom went on whitewashing—paid no attention to the steamboat. Ben stared a moment and then said: Hi'yi! *You're* up a stump, ain't you.... You got to work, hey?"

Ben Rogers was playing a game and Tom didn't join in. This is one of the few adventures in his life Tom Sawyer missed out on. He sure could have had a lot of fun if he had started waving around his paint brush on the back of the steamboat, shouting out seaman's lingo in response to the captain. Then he could have avoided being "up a stump." We also sure could have a lot of fun if we leaped onto the opportunities of play that life plops onto our laps every day.

He had been eight years upon a project for extracting sunbeams out of cucumbers, which were to be put into phials hermetically sealed, and let out to warm the air during raw inclement summers.

JONATHAN SWIFT
Gulliver's Travels, 'Voyage to Laputa'

FOUR

Projects

The kingdom of heaven is like a merchant looking for valuable pearls, who, when he happened to find a magnificent pearl, went out and sold everything he owned to buy it.

—Matthew 13:45-46

The merchant hoped the pearl was worth more than everything he owned, so his project was a big risk. It turned out that he made a small sacrifice compared to what he gained, so he had reason to rejoice. The prize was a treasure, meaning in life, a direction and a goal. It is the worthy answer to the question, "What am I going to do with my life?" Or

69

"To what can I dedicate myself?" When we feel low, often the reason is we have nothing we can call a worthy goal. It is a signal we need to mature into something bigger than ourselves, a higher kind of wellness.

For wellness we need meaning in our lives, more than something to do, more than making money, more than busy work. We need a project or more than one project, something that includes a goal, meaningful labor, satisfaction in doing it. That can be raising a child, planting a field, writing a book, working for a child's future, teaching school, racing sailboats, buying and selling, the whole range of human activities. If we are not doing what we are suited to be doing, or if our contributions are not appreciated, eventually we become unhappy, sometimes even anxious or depressed.

Whether we are looking for a project or deciding on a life's work, we first have to understand what we are good at and what makes us happy when we do it. Thoreau put it this way: "Cultivate the tree which you have found to bear fruit in your soil." Others can suggest ideas, but good projects will always be finally chosen by ourselves alone. Good projects make us feel like a kid again, get us excited, make us want to get back to it, become fun even if obstacles and hard work are involved. They put magic into our lives, a fire in our spirit, a glint into our eyes.

70

A good project is like a good spouse, a good friend, a good partner. It is liberating, that is, it can be an external force that helps liberate creative activity, joy, a sense of purpose, deep satisfaction. Of course, any good project will require hard work, discipline and include many obstacles and moments of frustration. But despite the great effort they take, we recognize good projects when we work on them instinctively because they provide us with many moments of exhilaration.

The problem with most projects, even wonderful projects, is the need to work with other people who have different ideas about how the project should go. Even worse is dealing with bureaucrats who are obsessed with meaningless procedures, or with people who seem to be working against the goals of the project. Even when we are convinced we are in the best position we can be, we become irritated with the need to deal with others. When we try to understand what the underlying difficulties are, try adjust to the sources of the problem, the experience can be maturing. We achieve a liberating perspective, even if we decide to move on to another project or job.

In any kind of work we have to learn that everyday stresses on the job are normal. We can learn to calm down in the face of tension, work with stresses, accept and adjust to them, setting up lines of communication. All big challenges present adversities, which can strengthen us and to which we can adapt ourselves. These are an integral and unavoidable part of living.

Working with other people on a project demands mutual trust, which comes slowly and needs patient nurturing. When strong trust comes to the team on a project, everyone knows it. Oarsmen on boat crews speak about the moment of "swing" when everyone is in complete synchronicity. Jazz musicians talk about being in a groove. These are the "high" moments of a race or musical improvisation because they are rarely achieved and bring feelings of complete satisfaction. There is a feeling for one another and a trust in one another that comes at that brief period. In all good projects trust can bring about a kind of "swing" or "groove" that feels like good music. That's what group effort is all about. It often takes a great deal of talking and working toward trust to reach that energizing peak.

We should try to do our best in all our endeavors in life but not expect others to notice them, applaud them, or even appreciate them. All people have their own problems, their own agendas. We can do only what we can do, work with the situation. We can't force issues, only work with each other, the gentler the better. Understanding our own personal limitations and agendas helps us to become more tolerant of others, who are in the same boat as we, with selfish interests as well as good will.

What we do in our lives involves a series of choices that may become more and more problematic. At first it might feel right to marry, to become "successful," to raise a family. Or we might want to work for the betterment of the world and the environment. We might want to detach ourselves from the world. Some of us try to do all of these things and more. Real life is messy and does not unfold before us with obvious decisions to make. We can only make one choice at a time and should be as honest as possible when we make it. We know that the best projects are not done only from a sense of duty, rather with a free and open decision.

Thinking about good projects is satisfying in itself. We get pleasure each time we complete a step or turn a bend in the stream. Whether aiming an axe and swinging, or completing a good paragraph, a sense of satisfaction can make one's day. Love of the project, hope in its completion, and laughter throughout the process, are rewards of a worthwhile project. Yet sometimes we become so obsessed with a project that we push to reach objectives overnight and end up in a state of exhaustion. Unreflective quick actions often cause big problems later. We need to slow down and <u>live one moment at a time, doing one thing, facing one problem at a time.</u> Only then can we enjoy the moment, trumpet the work, find delight in the project.

Projects enable us to focus on objects and people outside ourselves. When we concentrate on ourselves alone, what we have to accomplish for ourselves or how much money we have to make, we lose the feeling of inner freedom. Good projects are not dependent on outside approval, even when we are doing something good for others or working for the whole human environment or a great cause. Good work is its own reward.

When we concentrate on a project, we join in community with something bigger than ourselves. Our problems, our egoism and self-centeredness dissolve in the greater good. We need continually to be brought into the larger scheme of the world, its value and our relationship to it. The joy and satisfaction is in the doing because we tap into something larger, even in the smallest of tasks.

The good project is always informed by a spiritual center, our focus, desire, love. Whether tending roses, serving at a soup kitchen, carving out a block of wood, or teaching our child, we work with love and direction. In good work we hope and trust that all our lives will be better, happier. A good project is as often picked up intuitively because "it feels right," or "it struck me," as much as one planned for months.

An orchestra conductor once said that the most difficult instrument to play is second violin because the orchestra needs good harmony. He can always find first violin players, he said, but getting a second violin player who is excited about playing second fiddle is difficult. For harmony in the development and success of projects, the common good is more important than individual recognition. A lot of good second-fiddles are important.

Fine motives usually accompany our projects, whether making money for our families or feeding the poor. When we become obsessive about them, when we don't think about or do anything else, in short, when we are driven, we often neglect others, stop having fun and ruin our health. It's a common story in American culture. We live on the deferred payment plan in order to satisfy the urge to do. The fun should be in the doing, in the journey, in the here-and-now.

A potential problem looms with many projects, but not in the work itself. It comes with us, either in the difficulty in completing it or in our compulsive need to finish it. Some people never finish what they start, others are so driven to finish, their satisfaction is momentary. They're already on to something else, building up their identity or doing another good work that they hope will bring recognition or momentary satisfaction. All projects carry the seeds of workaholism, where peak performance is lost as well as the joy of creativity.

Too often we develop an impatient style of life that pushes us to complete projects ("good works") as fast as we can so we can get on to the next. While we are in the middle of Wednesday, we are looking forward to Friday's activity, on Friday looking to next week, or next month, or next year, and so on. We need to figure out why we are so driven, so impatient, so unable to wait for anyone or anything. If we do not, we'll never be able to enjoy our projects, the people around us, the fullness of our lives.

Striving to do good every minute of the day is connected to trying to be perfect in everything: taking extraordinary care of our families, overworking at the job, keeping the house neat as a pin. We can't seem to stand to leave anything in our charge undone, and thus create an anxiety in ourselves until it is completed. In this frame of mind, the only times we can be happy are when we complete a project, and then the satisfaction is short-lived. We have to practice leaving some chores undone and understand the world is not going to end. It doesn't make any difference how long it takes to finish many of our projects, and we certainly don't have to finish them overnight. We need to start a program of "wait-training."

Insisting on perfection for ourselves and others is an impossible goal and self-defeating effort. At bottom we pursue perfectionism because we measure our self-worth by our successes and cannot stand failure. Perfectionists have to learn that nobody is, or can be, perfect, and many mistakes will not ruin a project. Rather, we have to understand that mistakes help us learn and improve ourselves. We have to continue to do our best not think we are so god-like we'll never make mistakes.

Because we want everyone to like us, sometimes we take on projects for which we have no interest, time, energy, concern, or even talent. We need to learn to say 'no' to projects that don't fit us, so we can devote our energies to the projects that matter most to us.

One variety of perfectionism shows itself when we get into the habit of not finishing what we start. Our lives are cluttered with dozens of uncompleted projects. We deprive ourselves of the joy of finishing something, maybe because we are afraid of failing or doing an inadequate job because our expectations of ourselves and others are so unrealistic. Maybe our eyes are too big for the number of projects we get interested in, and just need some discipline about managing our time and saying "no" to some of our interests. Without strong efforts we are bound to fall deeper and deeper into this syndrome.

Projects are two-edged swords. On the one hand they can fulfill a need, such as personal recognition or becoming part of something larger than ourselves. At the same time they might become a source of great stress that can lead to illness. We like the recognition and feel we are doing good work but might not be able to handle the stress or uncreative aspects of the work. We have do decide whether we want to continue the project, whether we can (or want to) practice anxiety-relieving techniques like yoga, meditation, or breathing exercises. We may need to let go of the project. At the very least we should stop occasionally, clear our mind, and observe what's going on in our feelings and body.

The Tao Te Ching speaks of life as the flowing of a stream. We keep moving, splashing against and slipping around rocks, changing the physical composition of our bodies, cleansing ourselves, moving onward toward new environments. The rapid movement toward new projects and goals is exciting but also may be threatening if we are not grounded in the deeper self—the Tao—that feeds our spirit. With an abiding sense of a deeper reality comes the confidence to embrace ongoing changes in our lives.

One great value of projects is the opportunity to become aware of the present moment, to connect with the larger picture of life, to see beyond our simple actions. We can strengthen our inner freedom by doing something because of its own value, without regard for external rewards, fame or fortune. We know we are doing something good and are freely choosing to do it, thereby achieving harmony with our Highest Selves.

But then one is always excited by descriptions of money changing hands. It's much more fundamental than sex.

NIGEL DENNIS
Cards of Identity

FIVE

Money

*B*illionaire real-estate developer Donald Trump has commented often about the famous yacht he named the *Trump Princess after he bought it from Adnan Khashoggi, the reputed arms dealer. He provides detailed descriptions in* Trump: The Art of the Deal *about how shrewdly he bargained for the yacht and how good a deal it was. He brags about how he improved it in every way, in short, how he made it the greatest yacht in the world.*

Yet in his book Trump: Surviving the Top, *he informs us he's "giving up the game of who's got the best boat." The book came out shortly after his casino and other real-estate losses came close to bringing his financial empire into collapse. Because of his money woes, Trump stopped construction on the Trump Princess II, the $230 million yacht that was to replace the Trump Princess I, which he* *had to put up for sale. By the end of 1990, he couldn't afford either one anymore. Forbes magazine dropped his name in its annual ranking of the 400 richest Americans, saying that his "net worth may actually have dropped to zero."*

Donald Trump first seemed to say that buying and owning the biggest and best yacht didn't live up to his perception of complete fulfillment. Then his financial empire began to crumble, and his personal life took on new meaning. He began to talk about his next book where he would describe how he made some mistakes and came back to become the richest man in the country once again. Making money seemed to become an end in itself, not money to buy fame, fortune and power, but just to make more money than anyone else. He assumes that most of us spend most of our waking hours thinking about how to make money and offers himself as a model of how to do it.

Money, of course, is supposed to provide the means to happiness. Certainly it provides a more comfortable life for ourselves and our families, a good education, travel, some status, a bit of power. And many of us actually do possess this Trump quality of making money for money's sake, long after we have plenty to live on. Why are so many people so driven? Is it because of an innate greed that overpowers other more lofty goals? Is it so we can put the money to noble uses? Or is Donald Trump truly the model? Do we really believe his implied claim that making money for its own sake brings more thrills and joy than owning yachts, being president or a movie star, or anything else?

Even in the case of Donald Trump it is difficult to say what is need (at least psychological need) and what is greed. All of us have many material possessions we probably don't really need, more clothes and shoes, overly rich foods, more trinkets and playthings. We also have a tendency to want to look as if we are very up-to-date, know what's in and what's out, and all the rest. It comes down to what we feel we need and that feeling is a psychological problem. If we feel very needy, no amount of material accumulation will satisfy us. The old Latin maxim is appropriate: "Desire wants fulfillment; fulfillment wants desire." Life becomes a never-ending struggle to accumulate more and more possessions and achieve more honors, and in the process feel good about making money. But if we feel adequate and content about ourselves, there is no compulsion to jump on the accumulation merry-go-round or become addicted to the process of making money.

Money is associated with power and vanity because people believe money will bring power, and vanity is often the fuel that drives us for more money and power. With large amounts of money we begin to believe we can do anything, so we constantly overreach ourselves. Those who are in this position are highly publicized but the disease is common in all social classes and is highly contagious. It is infused throughout our culture.

An addict said he took drugs because they gave him a momentary high, a thrill that made him believe he could do anything, that he was "the man." The interviewer asked him if anything else could give him that kind of high. He responded, "yes, being in one of those skyscrapers, well-dressed, in my own office giving orders and spending money."

Although most of us do not fit into the Trump mold of money or status seeker, many of us share the assumptions of American culture. We try to get out there and make as much as we can. We develop a built-in calculator about what we earn, what we deserve to earn compared to other people who work less, how much we owe other people, and how much they owe us (especially the latter). The calculator includes items like goods we could buy if we had more money and how we would feel if we made a lot of money. We tend to develop a self-image based on what we have, whether or not we like to flaunt our status publicly.

Many of us are never sure we have enough money to get through the next depression, provide the best for our families, or enough to give us the status we think we need. More money does not give us automatic security. In fact more of it seems to increase the number of things we think we need and want.

Money is one of the biggest problems in life: the first is getting enough to live on. But as we reach financial security we begin to realize that, like life itself, money could be a temporary gift and not meant for hoarding. We should try to use it properly and enjoy it as one enjoys life itself, but not so much that it separates us from the rest of our fellow humans. We dearly understand that money increases our own enjoyment of life. When we work hard for it, we instinctively feel we have a right to use it any way we feel like using it. Money doesn't have to be, as the old song suggests, the root of all evil, but we know it can encourage selfishness, extravagance, even niggardliness.

There is no doubt that continually saving for some future prize cements a bad attitude of always living in the future rather than the present. Sometimes it's best to abandon frugality and spend money on a luxury we and our loved ones will enjoy right now—a lavish vacation or wonderful meal out. The rest of the time we can focus on saving for future necessities.

We realize that whatever we earn we can lose much faster than we earned it, so we put away as much surplus as possible for the future. In fact, getting people to spend money as fast as they make it is the economic aim of our society. We think we have enough to spend and save, enjoy life, take care of our children's needs and their wants, give to charity. Dealing with the conflict between spending and saving stays with most of us all our lives.

If we have enough to live on, the problem is to walk the path between hoarding and acquiring. We fear losing what we have earned, but we are driven to splurge because of psychological need—to accumulate things, to keep up with fads, to shop until we drop. The first hinders true enjoyment of life; the other is generated by the need to bolster ourselves up by material glitz. Meanwhile, the admen blitz us their "Enjoy yourself, it's later than you think," a warning to those in mid-life crisis. We need to strive for an inner freedom that allows us to make choices about our goods that are not fed by compulsion or outside pressure.

We know that money can't buy us happiness, but we act as though it will. We have to test the age-old truths for ourselves: to stop grasping for more, accumulating more, desiring and seeking for more than anything outside our immediate situations. We may earn more money or honors, but we know it would better to stop striving for them with all our energy. We would be better to stop continual maneuvering for better and more prestigious positions and try to curb our unrealistic ambitions. We won't know the truth of the adage until we live it.

Material success exists only in the minds of those who create the idea or ideal. These include the mass media, the "rich and famous," and the merchandisers who sell goods and services designed to lure others into the myths of material success. This fact is so blatant it is astounding how anyone falls for it, yet most of the world has bought completely into it. Everyone jumps on the "ladder of success" and climbs his heart out, as our lives become more and more complicated. We may not be able to uncomplicate the ravelings of the world around us, but we can learn to simplify our own personal lives. We can live on less and expand our sympathies to others.

We learn and develop legitimate desires for material comforts early in our lives, and we learn to bargain for the best deal. How many of these desires are natural and how much does the market economy drill them into us? It seems that material desires expand with growing income. We spend, cut the best deal, want more, cut better deals, buy better status for ourselves. Is any of this making us any richer? We know the answer to this question, yet stay right in the race for more things. "Things are in the saddle," Emerson warned.

According to many surveys, most people would lie if it would help them get money or other material gain. They also pretend to care about others more than they really do. It is easy to discount these studies or deny we would lie just for money. It is also possible to pretend to care about others more than we really do, simply because our society tells us we should. The truth is that most of us are quite attached to possessions and might be inclined to stretch the truth to increase them. Most of us think three or four times about ourselves before we consider the needs of others.

For many of us, guilt lies just under the surface. We feel we don't deserve what we have and wonder how much we should share. Feeling guilty is rarely helpful for anything, including sharing with others. We need to feel comfortable, not guilty, about whatever we do for other people. Money is the extension of our interest in other people.

There are takers and there are givers in the world. Most of us realize we are both takers and givers. We give because we realize how much we have received from others: family, teachers, friends, literature, and even the fleeting encounter. We need to give ourselves to others. Money makes sense only insofar as it is the personal extension of ourselves. If we try to develop our own deeper consciousness, simplify our desires, look at the deeper side of life, money might assume its proper subordinate role.

Creation is a representation of a great gift, and we share in the act of creation by daily actions. Money can be used for this purpose. Also it can be used to assuage our guilt. We can hoard it, or other people can bilk us into thinking we are using it for good, when it actually is building their personal empire. Goodness to others does not need money to give it status. Money can contaminate the good we try to do, and it can enhance our personal generosity. Rarely do we think about which role money really plays in our lives.

High calibre human beings—like fine china—may well contain a few flaws within their exquisite patterns.

JEAN DE LA LAFONTAINE
Fables

SIX

Encounters

There once lived a cranky old bureaucrat who tended to be disagreeable to his family, friends, clients, and anyone else who happened to cross his path. One day he was transformed completely into a kind and gentle person, who treated everyone he met with dignity and patience. Naturally his friends wanted to know how this change came about, and he explained,

"I used to spend all my time seeking happiness, then I decided I would settle for being content."

The stuff of life is rooted in brief or long-lasting encounters, meetings, relationships with other people. At bottom we will be happy or sad, fulfilled or unfulfilled, because of the way we relate to others, what we expect of others, and how they accept and relate to us. All our encounters from birth are the strands that make up the tapestry of our lives, showing bursts of primary and muted colors throughout its irregular design. Encounters show the process of our lives. They are etched in our memory, the fruits of our ideas and beliefs.

The people we live and work with or encounter every day are like ourselves. If we realize that relationships carry human foibles and flaws ("within their exquisite patterns," as LaFontaine put it), we are more able to shake off discontented feelings and achieve the (changing) state of contentment and well-being. Acceptance of human flaws, including our own, can bring more happiness than perfection, fame or fortune.

Fulfilling relationships or brief encounters all challenge us to greater maturity, wholeness, wellness. We are invited to meet another person, listen carefully, understand how he or she thinks, and respond with sensitivity. Very often we listen poorly, fail to understand, respond according to our moods and prejudices. We lose an opportunity to seal a bond with the world.

The encounters in our lives are made up of thousands of contacts with other people. There are solid touching points and mushy ones, happy ones and sad ones, dear loves and neutral associations, close friends and enemies, family and work, and many more. The challenge is to explore our encounters and seek to understand them, see how they enrich us or how we close ourselves off from others.

We cannot control our human environments, no matter how hard we try. The more we try to control or shape the contours of our relationships, the more we fall on our faces. We can only try to live with others, understand and respect them and their needs, work with them for a mutually better life.

Human encounters are changeable and often volatile. We might make an innocent comment which provokes a verbal attack from another. Someone questions our motives for no apparent reason. We are shaken, become angry, and avoid contact with the person. We are innocent and expect our antagonists to appreciate our innocence. Yet, our expectations can be as much of a problem as the attacker. We assume they look at us and the world with the same values we have, when in fact they undoubtedly have very different outlooks. Both sides of an encounter are burdened with attitudes, expectations, a lifetime of conditioning and beliefs that can destabilize a relationship. We expect too much of ourselves and tend to overlook the agenda others might have. Other people also look out for themselves and their own needs first. We can't expect them necessarily to understand how we feel when we are snubbed or insulted.

Our daily encounters can easily result in misunderstandings. It is remarkable that most relationships survive at all. We think we really know our friends, neighbors, fellow workers, and loved ones, especially when we have been around them for many years. Further we expect people to understand our moods, what we are thinking, when we have something on our minds, when we feel like talking, or the opposite. They don't always connect with us any more than we connect with them. The best way to cope with *mis*understandings is to realize how hard ordinary understandings are.

Thoreau once said we must impart our courage to others, and not our despair; our health and ease, not our disease. Our sickness (of body or mind) should not be allowed to extend outside ourselves.

When a friend says he will do something for us, and the friend does not, we naturally are disappointed—often angered—because we expected him or her to respond. The friend has his own set of priorities, might be thoughtless, got a better offer, or just didn't care about what we considered to be a solemn contract. This is the stuff of a big scene but shouldn't be. We probably developed unrealistic expectations about our friend. At least we can learn to appreciate the friend for as much as he or she wants to give. We certainly shouldn't ruin our day with a major self-righteous argument that becomes a lengthy feud.

Most of the time our misunderstandings or optimistic expectations that collapse are generated by commonplace frailties like thoughtlessness or forgetfulness rather than bad will or malice. Even if someone manifestly is showing bad will, we can gain valuable experience on when we should back off an encounter. All of us might have streaks of bad will, which may or may not show up, so we shouldn't be surprised when it appears in our lives.

We seem to gain or lose confidence in ourselves from our encounters. Other people might boost us up or tear us down, love us or hate us, admire or fear us. Most of all, we look at the world through the values, insecurities, beliefs, perceptions, and expectations we cultivate in ourselves or perceive coming from others. We program ourselves to react to other people according to the patterns of our beliefs or our instincts. If someone attacks us, we attack back; if someone loves us, we love back; if our insecurity engenders suspicions, we become aloof; to protect ourselves, we develop a thick skin. We seem destined to act or react in a predetermined way, but it need not be so, should not be so. We can pause, acknowledge our offended feelings, act or not act, wait. We have to accept responsibility for how we relate to others, especially how we handle our emotions during a crisis.

It is possible to accept criticism from others as friendly, although this is rarely considered. We can learn to accept criticisms or hurts from others as kicks in the behind, designed to wake us up. The "friendly criticism" assumption presumes another person's good will and forces us to consider the criticism as legitimate. If the criticism is a product of bad will, we can profit from it and try to develop a new relationship. If bad will was the cause, we can more easily pass over the sting, knowing we did our best to meet our adversary's challenge.

When we sincerely understand people we do not like or who have been antagonistic to us, we change our own capacity to respond to other people's needs. Furthermore, we might help our former enemy understand how it is possible for someone to respond to insults with compassion. Both sides can grow from the experience. Dostoyevsky paraphrased the Bible when he said "it is easy to condemn wrongdoers and very difficult to try to understand them."

Brief encounters sometimes grate the soul. We are cut off in traffic, or someone is rude at the office.

Bad encounters mount up, cause stress, fray our nerves. We can learn to accept insults with calm if we become less perfectionist, lower our expectations once in a while, realize modern life is rife with jarring moments. We need not shout back at someone who shouts at us, though it is an understandable response. If we allow our outbursts, we should then try to convert the anger to understanding, realize we live in an imperfect world. We need to learn to live with compassion rather than prejudice. Human wellness flourishes with such a choice.

May we not have high expectations of our loved ones and friends? Of course—if we do not demand perfection 24 hours a day. The danger of accepting limitations and lowering expectations is that we can become complacent about ourselves and cynical about others. We can sell everybody short, especially ourselves. We may expect ourselves to be perfect and are saddened when we don't live up to our own expectations. All of us have bad days or times of the day. We only need to continue to give our best and hope that others give theirs. It is silly to expect anyone to respond exactly the way we prefer all the time. Developing realistic expectations of ourselves and others is the beginning of wisdom.

One way to understand our values or attitudes is to ask ourselves what we demand of others and ourselves. Often we are unrealistic in our expectations. We expect to be understood, praised and loved by others. But we shouldn't be shocked when others do not lavish love and praise on us or do not meet our expectations.

All of us are subject to injustices in our daily lives. We sometimes feel cheated by salesmen, slandered by coworkers, insulted by superiors, and ridiculed from every corner. There is little we can do except carry on, do our best and wait for events to come around. Awareness of religious presence is one kind of solace during periods of emotional abjection, but we can find many ways to work our way through depression. If we are able to calm ourselves in meditation, we might see how our actions might sometimes hurt other people, and how we also need forgiveness.

When someone slights us, says something rude, or betrays us with a malicious word or deed, ugly feelings may well up. Anger, resentment, hurt, possibly hate, may quickly overcome a calm disposition and displace whatever good feelings we might have had. Anger and resentment can last for hours, days, months. They take on a life of their own in grudges and statements of self-justification. We feel the hurt anew each time we think of the action. Harboring anger makes us a double victim and often takes a toll on our bodies.

"Forgive us our trespasses, as we forgive those who trespass against us," the prayer teaches. So often said, so often ignored. Children who never forgive their parents, brothers, sisters; even spouses, who never speak to each other; family members who hold grudges for decades; these are common experiences. Forgiveness may be the most difficult act of love, because withholding forgiveness appears to be an act of justice carried out by a person who has been wronged. Yet the paradox is that trying to hurt a person by withholding forgiveness hurts us as much as the "enemy." Getting even leads to an indefinite cycle of retaliations. The original hurt may have been motivated by thoughtlessness, ignorance, immaturity or bad will. Nothing is bad enough to perpetuate bad feelings among family or loved ones for a lifetime. Forgiveness is transforming, healing, renewing.

Overcoming anger does not mean we can root it out of our emotional life. Sometimes anger is a proper response to injustice to ourselves or the deliberate affliction of harm on others. But before we are swept up into a maelstrom of emotional turmoil, we should think about the life of the perpetrator of our unhappiness. That person, not unlike ourselves, probably is protecting his or her vulnerability by attacking before he or she is attacked.

Irritability—impatience, becoming abrupt or sharp to others—quietly corrodes our character and the ability to enjoy life. It reveals our self-important immaturity, our expectation that others should conform to our personal standards of perfectionism, our schedules and plans. It shows our unwillingness to allow other people to proceed at their own pace at the check-out counter or at solving problems they find difficult. Worse, it points to our own prejudice or intolerance of other people's opinions and values.

Irritability and impatience have to be met with calm assessment of the real situation, putting things in perspective. What is really important here? What am I worried about? Why am I upset over nothing? What is the worst that can happen, being three minutes late? What immature need is provoking this irrational response? Most of all, what joy in life am I missing by my silly impatience. Too often we are upset by trivial affairs, things that don't matter. They just don't matter.

When people perpetrate evil, the proper response is action. Anger, when it rises, needs to be moderated with thoughtful, calm deliberation and positive action: "With whom should I cooperate?" "What are the most effective tactics?" rather than "how can I get even?" Anger serves a subordinate function of moving us to show love and support for victims of injustice, but no emotion should become an obsession, a corrosive habit. Positive personalities are built on positive, not negative, traits.

Anger usually provokes actions that are regretted. We are offended or cut off in traffic and we respond without thinking. Sometimes we blow up at something that seems offensive and do or say things without knowing the whole story. Frequently we realize that if we could calm down for a minute—even when cut off in traffic—our day would be improved, even though the other driver is patently offensive. Stopping to think, or "dropping it," after an insult makes good sense for our own health and peace of mind.

Hesitation is an antidote for anger. We should take a deep breath, bring the anger into our consciousness. We can transform anger into calm by thinking out the circumstances of the situation, and sitting patiently on the feeling. Anger tends to rear its ugly head over and over. We need to admit the feeling, admit its right to explode, but must practice as much patience as we can muster until things calm down.

When others deceive, cheat, or lie to us (sometimes over long periods), we are deeply upset when we realize the truth. We tried to listen sincerely to others with the result that we were taken down a path paved in deception. The situation leaves us feeling helpless. Yet the situation can make us stronger in our own determination to be honest. Society cannot exist without the assumption that most people deal with each other honestly. We know our own frailties and the deceptive words and actions we use to bolster our own egos, so we should try to understand these failings in others.

Becoming embarrassed is one of the most common experiences of growing up and never leaves us. We say something dumb in a crowd, and realize it almost as soon as it comes out of our mouths. We do something dumb and pound the steering wheel in exasperation at our stupidity. The feeling stays with us for too long, and even returns when we remember the event. It is the price we pay for awareness of what others might think of us and our desire to be well thought of. The only mature reaction is to admit our blunder and realize tomorrow is another day, too great a gift to spoil by dwelling on past silliness.

Sometimes we are drawn into "doing something dumb." We may overreact to a perceived insult and later realize it was an innocent remark. We are stuck with the memory of our childish reaction. Knowing that almost everyone makes these blunders rarely helps assuage the feeling. However, it does draw us into the common condition of human beings, who are known for doing many, many dumb things.

Occasionally we hear by the grapevine that someone said something insulting about us. We are hurt or angry. What hurts is that the remarks seem to be untrue. Since we spend so much of our lives discussing other people in conversations ranging from gossip to character assassination, it should not be surprising that others would do the same to us. Gossiping is so commonplace that we should take it for what it is: a low-life activity; not evil, just low-life. We should laugh about what comes out of gossip sessions, not take it seriously. In the context of everyday office conversation and the human proclivity to gossip, unkind comments should be expected. It seems to be part of human nature, to build ourselves up by tearing others down. It's humbling to know that few people escape the clutches of gossip.

Among the deepest joys of life are encounters that connect. They need not be long-lasting but often are. There need not be physical attraction, though often there is. Mostly a feeling of mutual understanding blooms, of openness, a soul-mate emerges. If a friendship or love develops, encounters are relaxed, trusting, intimate, mutually fulfilling, a partnership that enriches both sides equally. The wonderful thing about good friendships is that we need no preliminary formalities, no finding out about the other when we meet, even after years of being apart. Instantly we connect and can enjoy each other's presence—free to speak with no playing politics, censoring our thoughts or mincing words.

Marriage has often been compared to a roller-coaster: The person you sit next to has to be strong enough to hold onto during the steep dips and relaxed enough to giggle with when it's over. Mostly, however, the roller-coaster ride refers to the ups and downs of daily life. Shared living takes so long to get used to; this should be obvious. We are all so different and at the same time trying to live in intimacy with one another. If we didn't have problems and disputes, we could be accused of extraordinary blandness.

In the face of personal turmoil, we first need commitment, or determination to make a partnership work. This is the first line of defense of a shaky union. We also need a willingness to talk when communication is difficult; mutual sharing in the face of hurt; forgiveness for possible betrayals; consideration in small matters; affection and intimacy.... All are necessary for partnership, especially when a couple freely chooses to love one another again after a difficult period of time. All couples need to relearn that a partnership constantly is in flux. We must adjust to new circumstances, life changes, and ages. We are continually moving into new kinds of living, new challenges, none of them easy. For the journey we need loyalty, patience, compassion, enthusiasm, courtesy, and an understanding of what it means to love and be loved.

We need most of all to understand that living in the world is basically an effort to communicate, to understand, to meet other people in an atmosphere of trust. The basis for the trust is a common humanity that shares in a deeper common spiritual reality.

I cannot praise a fugitive and cloistered virtue, unexercised and unbreathed, that never sallies out and sees her adversary, but slinks out of the race, where that immortal garland is to be run for, not without dust and heat.

JOHN MILTON
Areopagitica

SEVEN

Virtue

*I*n one of his Socratic dialogues, <u>Protagoras</u>, Plato had
Protagoras recite a creation myth, telling us that when
humans were created, they suffered great disadvantages
as compared to other animals. Humans have no fur or
claws and only limited strength and speed along with
other physical problems, so it was difficult for humans to
conquer their natural enemies. To help them Prometheus
had to steal fire and the mechanical arts from the gods.
These gifts gave them the ability to make tools and weap-
ons, to grow food, build houses and defend themselves
against stronger creatures.

Even so, humans succumbed to the wild beasts because they were scattered, living in isolated, small groups.
When they came together in cities for mutual support,
they were abusive to one another, quarreling and fighting

*to near destruction because, as Protagoras put it, they
lacked political wisdom.*

*The art of political government was in the keeping of
Zeus, where Prometheus could not gain access. But in his
mercy, Zeus, "fearful that the entire race would be exter-
minated," sent Hermes with the gifts of "aidos," reverence
or the ability to act morally and rationally, and "dike," or
justice.*

*Hermes asked Zeus whether he should impart
justice and morality to only a few, as the gifts of the
arts are distributed, or to everyone. Zeus replied, "To
all..., for cities cannot exist, if only a few have justice
and morality...."*

In the history of western philosophy, virtue has
been understood as blending *aidos* and *dike*, the habit
of acting rationally, morally and fairly. Virtue is the
ability to act "reverently and fairly." It is the ability
to see and act beyond one's self interest, with the
courage to accept responsibility for one's action, not
blaming someone else for one's own actions. It is an
essential ingredient of wellness.

Unfortunately humans possess not only a sense
of justice, morality, and reverence, but also emotional constraints, built-in habits, and genetic pre-
dispositions of selfishness. We want to live in harmony, but like the ancients, tend also to be abusive
to each other. We are a mixture of good and bad,
compassion and selfishness, honesty and deceit. We
can recognize goodness and truth when we see it in

ourselves and others, and we can resolve to bring out the good and honesty in ourselves as best we can. The difficulty, as Thoreau once wrote, is uncovering the monster, which often is not where we think it is.

Like the ancients, every day we need to call up the basic virtues of reverence and fairness, moreover realize we never will lose all traces of selfishness and deceit. When we admit our inherent imperfections, we can relax about these foibles and move from "crisis to wellness" as a constant state of affairs. We can be grateful for the gifts of *aidos* and *dike* because of their wonderful leavening of daily life. With John Milton we can praise and attest to the courage one needs to muster them up.

Most of us were brought up to act "responsibly," that is, not to blame others for our own actions. Many of us, however, seem to be willing to blame our genes, our background, or other people for obvious personal failings. Here are a few excerpts from news clips from recent years:

* A burglar fell through a skylight and sued the person he was robbing for having an unsafe roof.
* A drunken driver sued his host for allowing him to get drunk.
* A murderer claimed a life of poverty caused him to hate and kill others.
* Defense lawyers successfully defend their clients by blaming bad genes or over-sugared fast food.

We don't choose many of the circumstances of our lives—whether and when we are born with bad or good genes, what our family backgrounds and living conditions are. Still, we can choose how we will live, virtuously or with selfishness, with courage or by giving up on life. Living with virtue assumes we are glad we are alive, to love, to work, to plan and enjoy the universe, We affirm life by choosing the best part of life.

A virtue is a "good habit," something a person has to work at. It is a willful acceptance of responsibility to do good. We develop virtues when we "respond to value," i.e., when we are "able to respond" (response-able> responsibility). The virtuous person accepts responsibility, doesn't blame other people or events when things go wrong. When we habitually look reality in the eye and accept our role in creating it and when we treat others fairly, we act virtuously. Virtue is an act of personal courage and the keystone of a strong society, where people are willing to live with trust in one another.

Responding to value takes many forms in everyday life: watching a gorgeous sunset with awe; appreciating the good acts of others or just seeing the good in others; noticing another's plight and attempting to help; seeing the good in ourselves; thinking out problems and trying to solve them fairly. The habit of responding to values like these is virtuous in the sense that we are responding to something with a larger meaning and purpose. We believe the value is God-like, valuable in itself.

Virtue connects value within us to value outside us, the "kingdom within" to the "kingdom without," i.e., the world outside with what we believe is divine, internal value. Virtuous acts integrate our personalities as they pull together warring factions of the world in a process the Bible refers to as building the kingdom of God. The value outside ourselves includes the entire body of creation— other people, creatures, and the world of nature.

We give many names to virtue—honesty, love, goodness, compassion, courage, integrity, truth, sincerity and many others—but they share a common connotation: simplicity, a directness of action. Virtue is not folded-back on itself, self-absorbed, sneaky or deceptive. It is not askew, as are lies, which betray an utter disregard of others. Virtue acts with the directness of an arrow shot toward the target because it becomes an ingrained habit. This characteristic is profoundly social because it sows the seeds of trust in a community. It is not an easy task for any of us.

Virtue grows as we develop relations with the world. Other people matter to us more and more, as we see the value in other people and their beliefs. We extend our hands to those outside us with simplicity and concern, with no demands or hidden agendas. In virtue is a willingness to stand with them in difficulty, trying to understand what they are going through. With this compassion our empathy can extend to non-human beings.

Virtue has traditionally been seen as countering the human tendency to work for one's selfish advantage. When we see an opportunity to promote ourselves at the expense of another, the natural reaction falls on our own behalf. But virtue can work for the good of all, ourselves included, in the process of bringing out our own sense of justice and fairness.

We sometimes get a glimpse of our own frayed virtue when we deal with those who have difficulty telling the truth. They say whatever suits their advantage, advances their position, or attacks another's. Worse, they believe their lies about themselves and others. Since we rarely check facts about our friends, coworkers, or salespeople—this would be impossible—we are sucked into the process. When the truth appears, we are confused, upset, angry. Yet all of us are more or less involved in protecting ourselves from the harsh light of the truth. We should not accept deception as a way of life, in ourselves or others, but we can be compassionate to those who weave a web of illusion around themselves. We realize we are prone to the same kind of deception.

It takes courage to be honest about ourselves. And it takes courage to be compassionate. If we meet a panhandler on the street but prefer to give money to food banks or soup kitchens, it is hard not to avert our gaze. We need not say anything about our charitable preferences. Surely, however, we can affirm the person's existence, wave and offer a smile, and wish the person well.

The more honest we try to be with others, the more we expect it from others. So we are more vulnerable to the machinations of people who would prey on our good will. Is honesty and simplicity worth the price we have to pay for what appears to be gullibility? For many of us living in a marketplace culture which rewards shrewdness and guile, the price of a virtuous life seems too high. We wait for the day we can afford to be honest and straightforward, maybe when we retire. That day may never arrive.

Why not just go along with the culture, live for the moment, for excitement, money, pleasures, whatever we can take from the world? It is difficult to grow in virtue, why fight the forces of society and the natural inclination "to take care of number one"? It's a free choice. We have a short life to live and must think about the best way we want to live it. What will give us and the people we love the deepest form of happiness? What kind of legacy do we want to leave? We need not even look into ourselves to find the answer, but rather think about the kind of people we admire. We don't look up to the selfish, deceptive, money-grubbing liars in the headlines, but rather the honest, compassionate, kind, committed people with humanitarian projects.

Since few of us are living saints, we should not berate ourselves for thinking of our own needs as well as others'. We are not necessarily helping others when we appear to sacrifice ourselves completely. We need to support our own simple desires and act upon them without guilt. Giving to others with simplicity assumes we act because of the value in the deed, not because others expect us to act the way they want us to act.

Since all virtues can be overdone—courage can become foolhardiness, love can smother another person, blind honesty can deeply hurt others—we need to think through our dealings with others. Compassion is not unthinking, but our decisions need always be accompanied by sensitivity and caring.

We can show virtue most regularly in our daily associations with everyone we meet. That is, we can practice small acts of courtesy, gentleness, treating people with a positive, upbeat attitude, in short, going out of our way for them. In these little ways we are acting virtuously, responding to the value of their being.

The virtue of compassion or love can be best understood by non-love, non-giving, non-caring, not being loved, not being part of the universe of sharing, of taking gifts and giving. "Birds do it, bees do it," all of nature shares, gives and takes, imitating the gift of creation. It takes a firm act of selfishness to reject love or not to return it to other created beings. It is almost impossible to stay out of the loop.

Love is a creative, active virtue that constantly reaches out. It responds to the value of life itself, a smaller value in favor of the greater Value of the universe. Jesus said that to gain eternal life we had to love God with our whole heart, soul, strength, and mind, and to love our neighbor as ourselves. In loving ourselves, our neighbors, the world, we also love God who lives in all things.

Religious thought—Christianity, Judaism, Taoism, Buddhism, Muhammadanism—turns the cultural notion of success, failure, loss on its head. Jesus, Mohammed, and Buddha told us we have to "lose" our life in order to find it, to love others and become the lowest servant if we would be great. We should count ourselves as the last if we would be first. Is this the way it works? At least these notions let us know there is another way to look at life, that worldly success need not be prized as the ultimate goal.

Religious sentiments do not make virtue simple. Jesus said, "Be as wily as serpents and simple as doves." Simplicity sometimes goes against our grain when we feel others are taking advantage of our good will. When we choose to help one person or cause, we automatically screen out other people and causes. Those who ask for our support know this. So they try to obtain it in whatever way they can— playing to guilt feelings (we have many material goods, they have few), overstating their difficulty, etc. Jesus' statement confirms the problem which can be resolved by deciding for ourselves what is the best course of action.

The first Taoist Lao Tse, writing several centuries before Jesus, was even more emphatic on the subject of true success. The "wise person" will succeed in life only if he does not "exist for himself." In this position he is imitating heaven and earth, which likewise exist for creatures in the universe. If humans will be great and successful, they must imitate the great, i.e., the greatness of the selfless source of Being in its giving us all creation to share. The term *humility* doesn't do justice to these beliefs.

These thoughts remind us that our love should extend to future generations, who will not be able to thank us personally. An environmental ethic challenges us to respond to the value of a cleaner, healthier environment for those in the world who come after we die, and to respect the value in nature itself. We are programmed to run roughshod over any natural being or object that stands in the way of 'progress.'

Lao Tse told us he had only three treasures to offer us: simplicity, patience, and compassion. Simplicity because the Way of Life acts in the world with simplicity, to which we should conform. Patience with both friends and enemies, because flexibility and softness reside at the core of the Way. And compassion, because with it we show our unity and bond with every living being.

Lao Tse exhorts us to become as tolerant and open as the sky, resolved and firm as a mountain, supple like a tree in the wind, and simple as a little flower. We travel with no destination in mind, making use of anything that life happens to bring to us, immersed in the wonder and awe of the Way. In Christianity, Tao or the Way conforms to the theological term, Logos, which also means the eternal Way and pattern, represented in the world as Jesus Christ.

The basis of virtue in many religions is the divine spark in us all. Buddhists bow to others because they see the divine presence in themselves bowing to the divine presence in others. Christians believe that they participate in the divine life of Christ. The sharing of Life itself is befitting of mutual respect, acknowledgment of others' existence.

Human kind is, properly speaking,
based on hope; it has no other possession
but hope; this world is emphatically the
place of hope.

THOMAS CARLYLE
Sartor Resartus

EIGHT

Hope

*T*he *Judeo-Christian creation story in the first chapters of Genesis sets the stage for the drama throughout the rest of the Bible. Man and woman are created in a luxuriant garden, comfortable and secure in the enjoyment of their environment. They only had to withhold their desire to eat from the tree of the knowledge of good and evil. Knowing good and evil, of course, is the most dangerous creative ability humans could have: knowing, reflecting on knowledge, and choosing good or evil based on knowledge.*

The first humans could not restrain themselves from this most human of all human qualities, knowing and choosing. Thus they lost their primeval innocence and had the original integrity of body, mind and spirit shattered into pieces. Deep in their hearts they remain in a state of crisis, hoping against hope for a return to that original completeness of soul and body.

In the creation story, hope is linked with the ability to know the best course back to paradise, and to choose that course. But the incompleteness of our knowledge, frailty of our emotions and weakness of the will, all conspire against us. The challenge of life is to bring ourselves into a deeper unity of body, mind, will, conscious and unconscious. The Bible story presents humans in existential predicaments. We all deal with everyday conflicts, living in crisis, and choosing bits and pieces of wellness as we mature.

In the story God warns the man and the woman not to eat of the tree of good and evil or they would die. But the serpent (who also was from God) told them they would not really die. He offered that "their eyes would be opened" and they would be "like God, knowing good and evil" (an assertion God confirms later in the chapter). Knowledge and choice of good and evil is a god-like quality, bringing sorrow and new crises but also creating opportunities for higher consciousness, life and wellness.

According to the creation myth conflicts between good and evil are in everyone. After the original decision, all humans were able to be conscious of the difference between the good and evil in themselves and others. Biblical hope promises a deeper unity within ourselves and with the rest of the world, also straining towards that unity. Our choices in life determine how our lives are formed, whether we are integrating ourselves or running away from challenges. Whether or not anyone understands or appreciates our choices, we become the result of how we decide to live our lives.

In our continual quest for the full life of the mythic garden, we rarely have clear-cut, black or white choices. They are usually gray areas, ambiguities demanding work on our part to clarify what is happening in our lives. This is true of our inner development as well as what will happen in the outer world. We have to make many decisions without knowing all the consequences of our choices. We have to learn to live with ambiguity, with ambivalence.

Hope itself is filled with ambiguity. Is it better to play it safe and be satisfied with present certainties, or move ahead into unknown waters? In the creation story, one side said, "Don't take a chance." The other said, "You'll be more fully human if you do." To be human is to live with ambiguity, to realize that nothing in life is clear-cut. We have to make decisions with unclear knowledge. In this atmosphere we have to decide what is significant and what is we will act or not act on this imperfect

The decision that is most closely related to hope is picking up and going on when everything seems to be going wrong. Hope challenges bad health, stupid errors, poor decisions, people urging us to quit, crushing demands on our time, unintentional hurts to others. <u>Life still goes on; we always have another chance.</u> We have to shake off doubts or uncertainty and press on based on our imperfect knowledge and the vision of the life we want to live. That is the way hope is lived. "There is one thing I know how to do," said St. Paul. "I drop everything I left behind... and press toward the mark." Philippians 3:13,14. Paul didn't ask for a risk-free, comfortable life, rather he plunged almost impetuously into his work, his vision of how to live.

When we develop an image of what is important in life, most things that worry us are put into a proper perspective. We are comforted by our hope for the future, our place in the universe, a realistic understanding of ourselves and our own limitations. They simply don't matter, in the large or short-term scheme of things. When we are pressed down with the many concerns of the day, we should place them in context with the more important realities, hopes and dreams of our lives. Success or failure in the little things doesn't matter at all. <u>The quality of our choices, our</u>

good will and our respect for ourselves and others do matter. These count for everything.

Hope is not wishful thinking or a belief that if we hope hard enough everything will turn out wonderfully in the end. It is not a deferred payment approach to the future, giving up present satisfactions for a certain happy future. Hope is action we take right now for a future we choose, with all the risks of choosing wrong. Sometimes we have to dive into deep waters without knowing how we will get out. We have to trust ourselves and love the risk of living life.

We hope for an integrated, fulfilled future, but we don't know many details about it in the present, so we should be anxious about it. Yesterdays are gone; the future is unknown. We only can concentrate on what is happening and what we can do for today without wasting energy on what we might have done or been or what evils might come tomorrow. "Don't think about tomorrow; tomorrow can think things out for itself. We have enough troubles to deal with today." Matthew 6:34 We need to throw all our energy and enthusiasm into what is happening right now.

On a more concrete level, hope is the heart's promise for the future. Things will get better. A person will come into my life. I'll make more money. I will be recognized. The next job will be more satisfying. And so on. <u>Hope is nature's way of keeping us going.</u> When our hopes are dashed too often, we become cynical. We gain confidence when our dreams come true. Sometimes we can make our dreams come true; sometimes we cannot—we never know. The optimists keep trying, but the cynics give up. There is a connection between our unconscious yearning for the unity of the paradise garden and our fragmented search and hope in our everyday lives. Our daily choices often stress the transitory, short-term fulfillments. So we need to think more about the deeper, long-term meaning of our choices.

Hope expresses the tension between where we are and where we want to be: poor and rich; rich and richer; sick and healthy; unnoticed and recognized; weak and powerful, and so on. We can see unfulfilled desires within ourselves, which we may or may not be able to do anything about. We may be unrealistic about our desires, but we hope anyway. We can hope and still be content with our present status. Tomorrow we may try something else, or decide not to.

Mature hope always tempers its desire with knowledge and realism. Hoping to become a movie star, or a great writer, or president of the nation, or even hoping for the perfect job—all are conditioned on thousands of realities beyond our control. We can hope and we can do our best, but we must also realize the improbabilities of our hopes and dreams. It is silly to blame fate when our highest hopes are dashed. We still can choose how we want to live, whether or not we are bathed in recognition or wealth.

How important it is to balance strong hope for the future with realistic expectations! Our society promises much for hard work and equal opportunity but keeps quiet about the narrow entrance into many arenas. We might not fit their expectation of the best applicant; there may be outright but unrecognized bias. There is always the chance, but the odds are long to reach the top. There is only one Olympic champion, though hundreds might have done their best to reach that goal, and possibly lost because of a stomach ache, a bad toe, a misstep. There is no reason to stop hoping, no reason to stop working, but always with an appreciation for the joys of life we already enjoy. The fortune cookie reads, "Enjoy each moment; happiness is now."

What is the flip-side of hope? Not despair, not hopelessness, not cynicism. Not having hope includes one or more of all of these. Non-hope means we lack the willingness or ability to choose the deepest good for ourselves. It is a tragic condition. Sometimes it comes from immaturity, deciding to get even with ourselves for not being perfect. Life often deals many desperate blows to infants and children. Sometimes it takes years, decades of love for them to develop enough trust in the people and events of life to be able to hope. These are heart-breaking stories, but we know that it seems to be possible to overcome the most gruesome cruelty with patience and love.

Hope is a creative energy and desire, but constancy—being happy with who we are, what we have and what choice we are making—is the foundation of a happy life. Hope can become skewed into a force that drives us to an unending restlessness, never content, always wanting more, or wanting to be somebody else, or not ever knowing what we want. We waste our lives cultivating ambitions of glory, prestige and power. We refuse to accept our lot in life. Hope is a healthy setting of goals, a virtue that first knows the limits of possibility and the necessity of humility and acceptance. Happiness depends on surrendering ourselves to the lives we are living, and on the hopeful possibilities for the future. First we must be content with the joys of the present.

We are tempted to shoot for the stars because we are dissatisfied with our work, our self images, our humdrum lives. We are missing the simple joys of almost every job—service to others, seeing good in them, carrying out a religious act, finding creative ways to work. Although our lives can be difficult, they are also filled with many daily pleasures. We should allow ourselves to enjoy raising a child, loving and being loved, being with friends, growing flowers and vegetables, performing good deeds. We realize we seem to be where we belong, where we have chosen to be.

The hope within us all contains the seed of much more than the present world can offer, i.e., the garden and the tree of life. Hope coexists with risk-taking. In the Bible story, humans opted for deeper consciousness over innocence and dependency. The result was new emotions that overwhelmed them and sent them into hiding. The Bible over and over stresses the need to make choices that put us in touch with the deeper reality of knowledge of good and evil, the god-life.

The result of our daily choices is the realization that good and evil define the human personality, and that knowledge helps us to make choices. We make bad choices but even these add to our experiences and deepen our consciousness. Running away from choices for fear of making the wrong decisions causes us to lose the deepest part of human existence. Being human means taking risks, not hiding in the false security of avoiding choices.

The biblical injunction, "Choose life," refers to recognizing the good and evil in the world and choosing the good. It is a call to commitment and a hope that our primordial paradise will return one day.

There is surely a piece of divinity in us,
something that was before the elements,
and owes no homage unto the sun.

T.E. BROWN
Religio Medici

NINE

Religion

*H*ow *can I escape your Spirit? Or flee from your Presence?*

If I ascend to the heavens, You are there; if I make my bed in hell, behold, you are there too.

If I fly on morning's wings, and find the ends of the sea, you will guide me and your right hand will cradle me.

If I say, Well, at least I can be hidden by the darkness, I find that the night surrounds me with light.

No, the darkness will never hide me from your breath; dark and light are the same thing to you.

—Psalm 139: 7-12

The Spirit contains all works and desires and all perfumes and all tastes. S/he enfolds the whole universe,

and in silence is loving to all. This is the Spirit that is in my heart, smaller than a grain of rice, or a grain of barley, or a grain of mustard seed.... This is the Spirit that is in my heart, greater than the earth, greater than the sky, greater than heaven itself, greater than all these worlds.
—Chandogya Upanishad

People who have a religious consciousness, regardless of the religion, believe they are somehow connected to the source of all life, furthermore that this union always has existed and cannot be destroyed. Thus, religious awareness claims through faith that everything which happens, including our most trivial thought or action, is bolstered by the entire force of the universe. The belief supports a deep inner freedom.

An abiding awareness of the divine presence requires faith. This belief is similar to the faith we have in many people and things—science, technology, the belief that things will work out in the long run. When we have accumulated thousands of experiences that suggest an unseen presence, our beginner's belief becomes strengthened. It becomes difficult to conceive of the splendors of creation without a creator. Belief offers meaning to thousands of otherwise meaningless events. It changes our lives, our deepest wellspring. Yet faith is a fragile companion in the sound and fury of our everyday lives.

134

With religion comes both an inner attitude and an outer behavior that fits the religion. In most cases we live according to our understanding of a natural or eternal law. The biblical commandments, Taoist, Buddhist, or Muslim injunctions, all from revered texts are believed to reflect eternal life. We read sacred texts for a deeper understanding of the meaning of life and also for consolation and as aids to show us how to live. Soon we are led apply their wisdom to our lives and they become part of us:

"To good people, I show goodness; to those who are not so good, I also show goodness." Tao Te Ching

"Love your enemies, bless those who curse you, do good to those who hate you." Matthew 5:44

The everyday newspaper brings up the eternal question: "Why does God do bad things to good people?" The teaching is in eastern religions as well as Christianity: God "makes his sun rise on the evil and the good, and sends the rain on the just and the unjust." Matthew 5:45 If God is present in the world, he cannot withdraw himself from the unseemly. Eastern religions have gods with both destroying swords and loving Buddhas. God doesn't play favorites.

An abiding awareness of divine presence in us ultimately leads to a belief in a deep harmony among humans, animals, all nature and the universe. Religion is simply an awareness of that harmony and an attempt to live it in our lives, despite conflicts, tensions and everyday strife. Religion means living in time and eternity at once. The sense of religion is dependent upon this abiding faith, that a frail creature simultaneously is in touch with divine life.

The absence of religion is life without faith, looking at the world without looking at the unseen, deeper connections of life. Faith expands our vision of the world, sees a power, a 'Tao,' or way of life that may be imitated. How do we begin to see the unseen, to develop faith? Who knows? It is the opposite of believing only what you can see on the surface.

Most religions have the notion of immanence, God-in-the-world, and transcendence, God-beyond-the-world. Some religions stress the transcendence of God (like the Muslim faith), others the divine immanence (like Buddhism). The first chapter of the Tao Te Ching says that if we can express the Way in words, it is not the Way. Despite this, the book also exhorts its readers to follow the Way within us all. The divine presence is both completely beyond human understanding, and yet so close as to be inextricably part of everything material. This is the mystery of religion. The deepest, and most real, part of human nature is divine, and yet this reality is beyond human understanding.

Religion in both East and West promises happiness to those with faith because it releases the inner power of divine life. It is the power of compassion and goodness, the deepest reality sustaining an abiding awareness of everything that matters in life. Religion is not for next year or after the kids are grown up, but for now.

The enduring paradox of religion is the theme of death and resurrection, the existence of evil and good side by side. How can religion promise happiness when suffering is given equal footing with joy? Because many parts of life—work, family life, marriage, risk, sickness, accidents—lead to an understanding that sustains a deeper happiness. Happiness is not found in transient experiences, creature comforts, or Saturday night fun. Deep, abiding satisfaction is more complex and subtle than a million advertisers could comprehend.

The Taoist 'ten thousand' earthly preoccupations lead us away from the unseen side of reality. Ritual helps us back: community celebration, habits of meditation. Tibetan Buddhist monks make and dye pills into which they chant the power of the 'Lord of the Dance,' the creative power of the universe. Believers eat the pills and share the divine power with monks chanting, dancing and playing musical instruments around them. Similarly, Christians are put in touch with the divine life within them by sharing the eucharistic banquet. African American worship infuses the celebration with singing and hand-clapping. The experience affirms the life of the unseen, becoming more aware of the Great and becoming more like the Great by being with the Great.

When we are alone in nature, whether in the center of some majestic chain of mountains, or by the rush of a stream, or overwhelmed by a flood of spring wildflowers in a meadow, we naturally fall into awe because of the wonders around us. Nature sparks the currents of universal Being to run through us, as Emerson has written.

Emerson's disciple, Henry David Thoreau, also wrote abundantly of God's presence in nature: "My profession is to be always on the alert to find God in nature, to know his lurking places, to attend all the oratories, the operas, in nature. To watch for, describe, all the divine features which I detect in nature. The motions everywhere in nature must surely be the circulations of God. The flowing waves, the running stream, the waving tree, the roving wind—whence else their infinite health and freedom. I can see nothing so proper and holy as the unceasing play and frolic in this bower God has built for us. The ears were made, not for such trivial uses as men are wont to suppose, but to hear celestial sounds. The eyes were not made for such groveling uses as they are now put to and worn out by, but to behold beauty now invisible. May we not *see* God? I will wait the breezes patiently, and grow as they shall determine, as comes of resting quietly in God's palm. I feel as if I could at any time resign my life and the responsibility into God's hands and become as innocent and free from care as a plant or a stone. When we would rest our spirits, we must recline on the Great Spirit."

It seems easier to see God in nature than in the unfolding events of our lives, or in the faces, words and needs of other people. Both Eastern and Western spirituality stresses the presence of God in other people, nature and activities around us, but events and others seem far removed from our notion of religion. Yet in the people and events of history, the mystery of God's presence in the world is universally affirmed. Holy people find their sainthood serving others. They have found the secret of life in finding eternity in the present, not striving for some delusory future goal.

People are comforted by a divine presence in the middle of tragedy and conflict. "Abide with me," we say with our forebearers; "lead kindly light." These sentiments of awe, admiration and love stay with us, even after thorough indoctrination from a materialist culture and a life centered on the materialist needs of daily life. "I will lift up my eyes to the hills, where my help comes from; my help comes from the Lord, who made heaven and earth." Religion invokes awe and admiration, all a source of confidence and comfort. Thoreau once said, "God could not be unkind to me if he should try. I have never got over my surprise that I should have been born into the most estimable place in all the world, and in the very nick of time too."

Death is the final act of life. One cannot think of life without death. We knew nothing before life; we know nothing in life about what happens after it. We fall naturally into thought about what might happen after we die, but even this notion contains with it the idea of the fullness of life. When we "walk in the shadow of death, we fear no evil," for God, who always is with us continues to support our lives and hopes.

We know so little about life and its infinite possibilities, that death seems to be nothing more than pushing open more doors of life and experience. A different kind of existence, of course, but life after death seems just as possible as nothing at all. Even the skeptic Socrates admitted that he was as certain of this as anything else in life.

There is always the grief of separation at death, the feeling we may never see those loved ones who leave us in death. Then again, we might all see each other in greater fullness. A wonderful thought, a wonderful hope. It is confirmed by our deepest feelings, a depth of conviction far more than wishful thinking.

God is in the details, the saying goes: in the smile to others; the act of service; difficult daily work; little pleasures, hardships, coping with illness, planning a better world. It helps to reflect on the many details that are the foundation of all religions.

When religion becomes a centering event in our lives, both inner and outer, we find a way to relate to this framework of living. We develop an attitude of becoming aware of what is happening to our inner lives. We tune our consciousness to the present, to what is going on around us, to seeing the gentle flow of the Tao or Spirit in our everyday lives. The eyes of faith recognize a reality beyond material forces outside us and a deeper reality within our consciousness. In the book of Genesis God asks Adam, "Where are you?" That's what we do in meditation, look within and outside ourselves to ask ourselves where we are and try to connect onto a reality or movement inside the surface of events.

Religious awareness does not happen without our concurrence. Sometimes in silence, in meditation; sometimes in a special awareness while we work or are active with others; when we walk or sit in the park. Religious awareness is happy because it is expectant, enjoying whatever comes. Even thinking in silence brings unexpected insights, and the silent meditation that quiets the mind and concentrates only on breathing provokes deep relaxation. Religious awareness is an oasis in the turmoil of modern life. Religion doesn't need ad men or the blare of trumpets.

Although the religious presence can occur in any activity, it does require discipline because of the pull of ordinary life. Setting aside specific times during the day to meditate or reflect on one's feelings or activities usually is required. We usually need to remind ourselves to expand our awareness beyond what we habitually focus on like family or work responsibilities. We need to look for things we don't usually look at, to develop fresher, deeper approaches. Spontaneity and openness are the key. Some people who follow an ancient practice in yoga walk with their palms outward and cupped. This shows acceptance of all they encounter.

There is an aspect of religious awareness that requires constant attention because it is so easily lost. In one of Jesus' parables, he speaks of the person who goes to his friend in the middle of the night. He asks his friend for bread and is sent away, but he keeps pounding on the door (Luke 11: 5-8). His friend finally gives him the loaves because of his persistence. We do not need to pound so hard on our own door but should continually return to a source of great energy for ourselves.

The ways of religious awareness and meditation are many. They include thinking about an obsession or a disturbing or happy feeling to find its source; focusing on breathing and finding a relaxed rhythm; awareness of tension in the body and relaxing it; quiet sitting or lying down; listening to music to quiet oneself. Religious awareness also includes communicating with all parts of our nature, within and without, to our deepest reality. Sometimes we need to verbalize our sorrow or our joy to loosen a deep-seated guilt feeling. Other times we want to express admiration and awe for a power we recognize as greater than we have ever known. The religious awareness becomes our most profound expression of responding to Value in our lives. It recognizes the presence of grace, a movement greater than ourselves and power beyond anything in our experience. Here, too, is a commitment to choose the way that has been opened to us.

The final goal of meditation is mystic or divine union when our minds are quiet without random thoughts and feelings constantly demanding attention. The consciousness is silent, captivated by the mystery of mysteries, "the flight of the alone to the

Alone," as Plotinus explained. In itself the experience cannot be described, but mystics from all periods of history proclaim that it is overwhelmingly
exhilarating, joyous, life-affirming and life-trans-
forming. The fourteenth century German mystic
Meister Eckhard declared: "Divine union brings
strength, wisdom, understanding and undescribable
happiness. We become focused in everything we do,
singleminded in our compassion and love, not overcome by wayward feelings, good or bad. We come to
know ourselves and God in his essential being."

The late well-known Buddhist teacher Shunryu
Suzuki liked to say religion is everywhere. Today it
is raining; that is religion. Now the sun shines; that
is religion. His simple message, expressed in hundreds of ways, was that the divine power is everywhere, in the universe, nature, the weather, in each
person. All we need to do is assent to it. Today I feel
good; that's religion. When I feel bad, that's religion.
When I win and when I lose, that's religion. The
traffic is a mess (or flowing wonderfully); that's
religion. My spouse is hard to live with (or my
greatest joy); that's religion. I can't stand my job (or
it's wonderful); that too is religion. The idea can be
multiplied infinitely, and makes a wonderful meditation. The dying priest in George Bernanos' grip-
ping *Diary of a Country Priest* places his last, joyous
entry into his diary: "Grace is everywhere," the
sentiment that resolved his despairing, crisis-ridden

life in a provincial village. Mohammed (like Jesus or Lao Tsu or Bodhidharma) put it this way: "Wherever you turn is God's face."

To see a World in a Grain of Sand
And a Heaven in a Wild Flower
Hold Infinity in the palm of your hand
And Eternity in an hour.

WILLIAM BLAKE
Auguries of Innocence

Afterward:
Six Traditions of
Religious Meditation

Prayers, Devotions, Rituals

Religious devotions in all religions are the prayers and rituals by which we express our reverence and love for God or his saints. We also take refuge and seek counsel with supplications for help to overcome difficulties in life, for our family and friends, for national and world concerns, for peace. With these rituals and prayers we commemorate cycles of life—birth, adulthood, marriage, sickness, death—and seek to join our personal lives with the divine power that infuses the universe. Devotional prac-

147

tices are personal and communal. Christian churches, Jewish synagogues, Buddhist and Shinto shrines, Muslim mosques, Taoist or Hindu temples all attest to this most common and universal way of divine communion, the deep acceptance of the divine presence in our lives.

Through these practices, called 'bhakti yoga' by Buddhists, we seek to achieve loving abandonment to, and a 'divine embrace' with God. This is the final purpose of all forms of meditation, whether we read the Bible, prayer books, the Tao Te Ching, or other religious books. If you substitute the Christian term for the divine principle, the *Logos*, for Tao (also an ancient understanding for the source of all life) while reading the Tao Te Ching, the book reads remarkably like the New Testament.

Holy Words and Sounds

The practice of chanting or reciting holy words or sounds over and over is most commonly found in Eastern religions, particularly Buddhism, Hinduism and Sufism. In the Christian Orthodox tradition, the prayer of the heart or 'Jesus' prayer is similar. By repeating the Lord's name, the divine presence and adoration is believed to be intensified. Other sacred sayings for Christians are 'Come, Lord Jesus,' or 'Maranatha,' chanted by the early Christian church during liturgical celebrations.

The words or sounds are often referred to as a 'mantra.' The Maharishi Mahesh Yogi from India has popularized this method, which he calls Transcendental Meditation, or TM, around the world. TM does not require that the person need to concentrate on the meaning of the mantra, which can be a meaningless but personally transmitted phrase or set of sounds. Simply repeating the personal mantra is said to lead a person into a transcendental experience with the intelligence underlying all reality.

Other Buddhist traditions, or chanting in tribal rituals, suggest focusing on one's words and chanting sounds as a way to drive away distractions and allow the mind to empty itself. When the mind is empty and at peace, the person is able to touch and feel the divine presence in acceptance, awe, admiration, and gratitude. Buddhists call their practice 'mantra yoga,' where the practice of chanting or humming, either aloud or silently, are supports for contemplation. (This is called *dhylana* in Sanskrit referring to the moment in contemplative meditation when the mind stops thinking its thoughts and becomes one with the source of all being.) Their sitting posture while meditating is part of a pyschophysical exercise system called 'hatha yoga.' The term 'yoga' itself refers to union with the divine source of life. Yoga emphasizes the methods by which a person becomes psychologically in touch with the absolute being, and simultaneously with all beings in the universe.

Purification of Experience
This Buddhist technique, called Vipassana medi-

tation, is designed to purge negative experiences like anger, hostility, feelings of hurt, pain and penetrate to the ultimate truth of all being. The understanding is that all our internal negativities find their external expression in our breathing and other parts of the body. We should first breathe deeply and concentrate on our breathing. Then, as our mind is attracted to a particular part of our body, such as tension in our stomach or heart, we focus on that part. We change our focus as the mind is diverted to another part of the body, or even the entire body. If we are distracted by thoughts, we should focus on the thought. Each time we focus we identify the part of body or thought and consciously let it "dance its dance" and pass away. That is, first we focus on a part of the body or thought, then consciously give a particular bodily tension or thought or feeling permission to exist. With the passing of the focus and permission, the problem of anger or negativity also disappears momentarily. The ultimate effect is the awareness of the impermanence of our thoughts and experiences and the abiding truth of the divine presence which never leaves us. We may greet this recognition with gratitude and awe. We learn to accept that presence as it expresses itself in our thoughts, feelings, and events as they occur in our lives.

Good Will and Friendliness

The awareness of the impermanence of disappointments and desires reminds us of the reality and

permanence of the divine presence and our con-
comitant feelings of gratitude, love and good will.
After formal meditation we can continue the feeling
by opening our consciousness to the 'divine embrace'. We let its smile radiate through the entire
body, section by section, until we are filled with a
mass of smiling energy. We then can express this
feeling to everyone we meet during the day. We soon
realize that they, too, are united with us in the union
of the divine spirit.

In the Buddhist tradition, particularly Tibetan
Buddhism, first we experience discomfort by focusing and letting it go. Then we generate feelings of
love and good will and keep returning to them as we
interact with other people throughout the day. In the
Christian tradition, we realize the presence of grace
or the divine life of Christ within us and express that
love and smiling energy in our lives.

Daily Work and Activities

For the Buddhists, 'karma yoga' refers to a
person's works or deeds, his everyday life, trade,
career, even play—all the actions by which we define
ourselves. Our karma is the way we do our work and
the way we live. No one is in charge of our karma
except ourselves. That is what we mean when we say
that what happens to us is our karma. We choose
karma and are responsible for it.

Both Buddhists and Christians traditionally have
thought of their work as a prayer. Buddhists and
Christian monks have taught us the value of settling

into our work, not thinking of other things while working. They encourage sidestepping distractions and enjoying the simple actions themselves, like doing dishes, or gardening, or manual labor. As we grow in the awareness of the divine presence, we can bring this spirit of meditation to more complex projects and activities. We find more and more fulfillment in the activity itself, rather than working to seek rewards or praise. The center of the work is not personal ego but rather the sense of merging the work with God.

Religion research expert Joseph Campbell illustrated that the spirituality of all religions is centered in the quest to "follow your bliss." It means finding what our innermost selves lead us to do. The process inevitably fascinates us, makes us feel deeply and vibrantly alive because it emerges from our awareness of and union with the divine. It is the source of our abiding joy.

Way of Acceptance

Human life is characterized by tension. We experience a dividedness or separation of inner life from outer, person from person, intellect from emotions, and humans from nature. There is also tension in the moral arenas of good and evil. Life is a struggle to stay poised in equilibrium, control (or run from) evils, and work for a better world individually and collectively. The way of acceptance is reflection on the need to accept life in all of its expressions, living and dying, loving and hating, fortune and misfortune, happiness and tragedy.

Christian religions have understood the world in terms of Jesus' suffering and death and his resurrection, or passing from the slavery of human bondage into new life. This belief was built on Jewish sacred history, especially their release from slavery in Egypt and passage into new life in the promised land. Eastern religions like Taoism, Hinduism, and Buddhism understand humans as already possessing the divine principle. We experience impermanence in the rising and fading of negativities (Buddhism); the struggle between the female and male opposites of the Yin and Yang (Taoism); or the dozens of clashing good and evil divinities representing pain, evil, and destruction as well as health, gentleness, and peace (Hinduism).

This meditation combines elements of several of those described above. The way of acceptance allows the pain and sufferings of life as in the purification of experience through Vipassana meditation. It transforms the negativities of life into good will and love. One experiences the emergence from struggle into the Joy by understanding the divine presence in ourselves, other people, and all life in the universe. It takes discipline to perform humble tasks as cosmic history, as a movement of the divine into the future. This has been described variously as 'karma yoga,' or as Christ building a new kingdom through our own and other people's activity. Most of all, it is our way of acceptance of the world. This means more than simply tolerating the dark side of life. Rather, it is our giving ourselves completely to it, embracing death and resurrection, impermanence, and the clash of opposites. Ultimately we are joined to the primal source of life and love. All religions present this human condition as their central belief.

Finally

Teachers of meditation emphasize that what we consider to be distracting thoughts are common during meditation and everyday life. Teachers thus direct the meditator to calmly return to the simple process that leads to awareness of the divine presence. Many types of meditation, such as Vipassana, speak of thoughts or feelings only as positive expressions of the reality of the divine presence. We are taught to accept these just as we accept external events and work with both positive and negative forces in our lives. Our minds are restlessly active at all times, and distractions can help us understand the deepest reality about ourselves and the world. That random thoughts have their own purposes should not cause us any distress even during meditation.

The ultimate result of quiet meditation or deeper awareness while living our daily lives is a profound happiness, though not necessarily continuing contentment. Human lives necessarily are filled with limitations, disease, pain, unhappiness, and negativities. "Following our bliss" means the joy of finding our life's purpose, and daily problems are dissipated in an ocean of bliss. Our focus is centered into the core of our being where we feel united to the power that moves the universe. Compared to that union nothing, no difficulty, finally can destroy this harmony with Life or our confidence in it. We lead our lives according to our abiding religious awareness and relate to other people and to the world in a way that reflects our religious belief.

Meditation, then, finally comes down to a split-second of spiritual recognition with our response of the wonder, gratitude, and a sense of joyful inner freedom. We need only to realize where we come from.

For Further Reading on Meditation

Carrington, Patricia. *Freedom in Meditation*. New York: Doubleday, 1977.

Goleman, Daniel. *The Varieties of Meditative Experience*. New York: E. P. Putnam, 1977.

Humphries, Christmas. *Concentration and Meditation*. New York: Penguin, 1968.

LeShan, Lawrence. *How to Meditate*. New York: Bantam, 1975.

Trungpa, Chogyam. *Meditation in Action*. Berkeley: Shambhala, 1970.

FINIS

About the Author

Joseph Petulla was born in Oil City, Pennsylvania in 1932. He studied philosophy and religion at St. Bonaventure University and the University of Notre Dame and received an interdisciplinary Ph.D. at the Graduate Theological Union and the University of California at Berkeley. Since 1958 he has worked as a clergyman, counsellor, and has taught philosophy, religion, humanities, urban studies, and environmental studies at six colleges and universities. Presently he teaches environmental studies at the University of San Francisco.

Dr. Petulla wrote four books in a Religion and Life textbook series during the 1960's, and since receiving his Ph.D. in 1971 he has written *Christian Political Theology*; *American Environmental History*; *American Environmentalism: Values, Tactics, Priorities*; and *Environmental Protection in the United States: Industry, Agencies, Environmentalists*.

The occasion for the writing of *Crisis to Wellness* was an illness the author contracted in 1988. He is married and has lived in Berkeley, California since 1968.

Journal Notes:

Journal Notes:

Reader: Review This Book!

Use this opportunity to talk to the author. Please forward any comments to COMMUNITY RESOURCE INSTITUTE PRESS, 1442-A Walnut #51, Berkeley, California 94709. Phone (510) 525-9663.

Rate this book's content (CIRCLE ONE: Excellent; Good; Fair; Poor)

Rate this book's writing style (CIRCLE ONE: Excellent; Good; Fair; Poor)

Will it be useful to you? (CIRCLE ONE: Excellent; Good; Fair; Poor)

What was your favorite part?

What would you change or delete?

What ideas would you like to see explored in more depth?

(Please photocopy and remit)

Crisis to Wellness • Book Order Form

Ask your local bookstore to special-order additional copies of *Crisis to Wellness,* or order direct from the publisher. Please inquire about quantity discounts when ordering 5 copies or more:

Please send me_____ copies @ $9.95 $_____
Postage and handling, add $2 per order   2.00
(Save money by ordering multiple copies)   _____
CA residents, add applicable sales tax or $0.83/book   _____
CHECK OR MONEY ORDER ENCLOSED: $_____

Order with credit card by mail or phone (510) 525-9663:
VISA, MasterCard or AMEX #_____ Exp._____

Name_____
Mailing Address_____
City_____ State_____ Zip_____ Phone_____

Mail to COMMUNITY RESOURCE INSTITUTE PRESS
1442-A Walnut #51, Berkeley, CA 94709 (510) 525-9663